Nonverbal Behavior and Social Psychology

PERSPECTIVES IN SOCIAL PSYCHOLOGY

A Series of Texts and Monographs • Edited by Elliot Aronson

A Continuation Order Plan is available for this series. A continuation order will bring delivery of each new volume immediately upon publication. Volumes are billed only upon actual shipment. For further information please contact the publisher.

Nonverbal Behavior and Social Psychology

Richard Heslin

Purdue University
West Lafayette, Indiana

and

Miles L. Patterson

University of Missouri
St. Louis, Missouri

Plenum Press • New York and London

Library of Congress Cataloging in Publication Data

Heslin, Richard.
    Nonverbal behavior and social psychology.

    (Perspectives in social psychology)
    Bibliography: p.
    Includes index
    1. Social psychology. 2. Nonverbal communication. I. Patterson, Miles L. II.
Title. III. Series.
HM258.H465 1982   320.2′22   82-11223
ISBN 0-306-40952-6

© 1982 Plenum Press, New York
A Division of Plenum Publishing Corporation
233 Spring Street, New York, N.Y. 10013

Printed in the United States of America

To
our parents,
our wives, Marsha and Dianne,
and our children,
Bruce, Tracy, Paul, and Andrea
and Kevin

Preface

Nonverbal behavior is most commonly discussed in terms of its separate channels or modalities, that is, one chapter on distance, another on gaze, a third on facial expression, and so forth. Representative of this approach are a text by Knapp (1978), Harper, Wiens, and Matarazzo's (1978) scholarly review, Weitz's (1979) book of readings, and Siegman and Feldstein's (1978) edited volume of chapters by prominent researchers.

This book examines nonverbal behavior from a different perspective. It is organized around those dominant themes in social psychology which have particular relevance for nonverbal behavior. Obviously, not all of the major topics in social psychology are represented here, but many receive some coverage in one or more of the chapters. The following areas are those having broad chapter coverage: (1) research approaches, (2) attraction, (3) social influence, (4) social regulation, (5) emotions, (6) individual and group differences, and (7) theoretical and applied issues.

By organizing this book around major issues in social psychology instead of simply covering each channel sequentially, we are hoping to provide some insights into important social psychological phenomena and their relationships to patterns of nonverbal behavior. It has been said that in studying nonverbal behavior you learn less about the nonverbal behavior than about people and how they respond in various situations. It is our hope that this book will provide the reader with an opportunity to learn about both. Furthermore, in developing these discussions across channels, we can analyze these social processes in a fashion more representative of the way they occur in the real world; for example, emotion is discussed as it is manifested in integrated behavioral patterns. At this point it may be useful to go over the organization of the book.

Chapter 1, "Design Issues in the Study of Nonverbal Behavior," focuses on questions of research design and methodology critical for the study of nonverbal behavior. Some of the questions faced by researchers in this field concern whether one should deal with the encoding of ideas or feelings into nonverbal behavior or the decoding of nonverbal behavior into the internal states implied by them. In addition to problems of strategy are problems of appropriate response measures, both for the nonverbal behavior and for other potentially related reactions.

Chapter 2, "Nonverbal Aspects of Attraction," first briefly discusses some determinants and correlates of attraction and then moves into a consideration of the role of nonverbal behavior in attraction. The degree to which there is symmetry between different kinds of nonverbal behavior and liking is also examined.

Chapter 3, "The Role of Nonverbal Cues in Social Influence," deals with a variety of behaviors contributing to social influence. The impact of nonverbal behavior on issues like deception, speaker effectiveness, attitude change, and helping behavior is discussed.

Chapter 4, "Nonverbal Behavior and the Regulation of Everyday Life," deals with a topic that has not commonly been considered a major area of social psychology. However, there are signs that a concern with the processes of social relations, the subtle and relatively minor adjustments people make to accommodate one another and protect themselves, are becoming more important in the field. This may be the result of the recent research by investigators in the area of human ethology. This chapter discusses how we regulate our level of involvement with others through the course of an interaction, from an initial greeting to a final departure.

Chapter 5, "Emotions and Nonverbal Behavior," is introduced by a short review of contrasting approaches to emotional behavior, including those of James, Cannon, Schachter, and Mandler. Next we discuss nonverbal behavior as indicators of emotionality. Finally, we analyze the research on nonverbal intimacy exchange and describe a theory explaining the patterns of nonverbal exchange.

Chapter 6, "Individual and Group Differences in Nonverbal Behavior," analyzes the influence of culture, sex, and personality on nonverbal behavior. We included this chapter because of the tendency of social psychologists to emphasize social or situational variables at the expense of individual and group differences.

Finally, Chapter 7, "Theoretical Integrations and Practical Applications," reviews some of the major theoretical approaches and proposes a comprehensive model of nonverbal exchange. In addition, specific practical applications of our knowledge of nonverbal behavior are discussed.

RICHARD HESLIN
MILES L. PATTERSON

CONTENTS

CHAPTER 1

Design Issues in the Study of Nonverbal Behavior

Planning, executing, and evaluating a research project, whether it is a relatively simple single study or a complicated string of related investigations, can be viewed as a series of related decision processes. The value and impact of the final product is often considerably determined by the early decisions on how to structure a research question. In this chapter we hope not only to show how important these various decisions are but also to provide a general framework for making these decisions. We certainly do not expect that most of the readers will become actively involved in research in nonverbal behavior, but most will be occasionally stimulated to wonder how a research problem develops or question the legitimacy of some of the results and conclusions reported in this volume. We hope that some may even develop their own speculations or hypotheses on various topics throughout this book. It is our belief that exercising this kind of questioning attitude is one of the best ways for the reader to maximize his or her gains from our discussions. The following presentation on design, methodology, and strategies of research should promote a better understanding of the basic decisions in the research process and make it easier to evaluate the merit and importance of various findings in the area of nonverbal behavior.

It is not our intention to go into a detailed discussion of design and methodology principles, but rather to cover enough of the basics to facilitate their application to particular problems in researching nonverbal behavior. First, we will discuss briefly the issues of validity, ethics, and design decisions. Next, we will cover differing strategies of research on nonverbal behavior and the variety in response measures available to researchers. Finally, we will conclude with a case study example in the planning and conducting of research.

VALIDITY

The issue of validity in research basically refers to the degree to which the measures used in a given study represent the processes and constructs of concern to the researcher. Perhaps the most crucial aspect in any research endeavor is that of *construct validity*. The focal concern of construct validity is determining if a construct is actually measured by the operations employed in a particular study. For example, if we were trying to assess the degree of attraction between individuals we might use any one or more of a number of measures such as self-reported attraction, frequency of smiles or touching, amount of mutual eye contact, total time spent together, ratings or judgments by friends, and so forth. Any single measure is certainly fallible; for example, smiling often increases when one is uncomfortable or trying to deceive another, and thus increased smiling alone would not reliably indicate attraction. However, to the extent that separate measures converge in indicating a common overall pattern, greater confidence can be had in a construct's validity. In general, it might be recommended that multiple measures be used to establish the validity of a construct (Campbell & Fiske, 1959; Webb, Campbell, Schwartz, & Sechrest, 1966).

A second component of validity is that of *internal validity*. The issue of internal validity focuses on whether or not a study is designed well enough to determine confidently the presence or absence of particular effects. In general, experimental designs which are adequately controlled and free of confounding influences provide a high degree of internal validity. Observational and correlational designs are more susceptible to confounding influences and are likely to provide a relatively lower level of internal validity. That is, in general we might have greater confidence in the conclusions generated from a well-designed experiment than from a well-designed observational or correlational study.

A third component of validity is that of *external validity* or generalizability. In other words, to what extent can the results of a given study be generalized to broader populations and to more diverse circumstances? For example, do the results observed in a particular laboratory study of nonverbal interaction employing college students as subjects apply to the "real world," where most people are not college students and laboratories are not common settings for interaction? Very often the internal validity of a study is insured by controlling the research setting to such a degree that the external validity is actually lessened. In recent years there has been a greater sensitivity to concerns about external validity, which, in turn, has led to an increase in research in the field (i.e., in natural settings such as libraries, bars, parks, waiting rooms, etc.).

From our discussion of this topic, it is clear that effectively balancing the issues of construct, internal, and external validity is difficult. Yet it is a critical starting point for developing a meaningful and successful research project. This goal is further complicated by the researcher's concern with ethical standards in conducting research.

ETHICS

There are a number of goals which the responsible researcher must meet in conducting research. The most obvious concern is that the planned research should not present any physical or psychological harm to the subjects. In contrast to some medical research, negative physical consequences to the subjects are very unlikely in most psychological research. However, some psychological or emotional effects such as anxiety, guilt, or embarassment may result from specific circumstances or manipulations in various research projects. A second ethical constraint is the need to inform subjects of the nature of the research and seek their consent to be in the study. Related to this is a broader concern, that of invading the privacy of subjects. In other words, how far can a researcher go in observing the behavior of subjects or in gathering information about them? A final matter focuses on the use of deception in research. On the one hand the pursuit of research questions very often requires that subjects be naive, that is, unaware of the true purpose of the study. On the other hand the researcher has an ethical obligation to obtain informed consent from participants in the study. In such cases, the researcher should fully inform subjects after their participation is completed.

These ethical concerns frequently present a kind of dilemma to the researcher. In general, preventing harm to subject, permitting informed consent, insuring reasonable privacy, and avoiding deception are goals that a researcher must pursue. However, these goals are not absolute. They must be weighed against the importance of the research, the possibility of pursuing the question in an alternate fashion, the degree of potential harm or inconvenience to the subject, and the nature of the procedures instituted to protect the subject.

Although this discussion provides a brief overview of some of the major ethical issues, the American Psychological Association (1973) has published a detailed guide on ethical principles with which investigators doing research on human subjects should be familiar. A final point which should be mentioned on the matter of ethical principles is that the decision about the propriety of a given research plan no longer rests solely with the researcher. Researchers in colleges and universities, in research institutes, or in hospitals typically must have their research proposals evaluated by a disinterested ethics committee. Only after such a committee is satisfied with the proposed treatment of subjects may the project begin. In addition, both federal and private funding agencies closely consider the ethics of proposed research programs before providing support for research.

STRATEGIES

It is now time to move to design issues that are more specifically relevant to research on nonverbal behavior. Our first concern here will be with differing strategies of research. We will use the term *strategy* to refer to the broad approach taken in studying nonverbal social behavior, whether it is an inquiry about attraction, emotions, or interpersonal influence. In addition, a consideration of different strategies will be independent of specific techniques, manipulations, or variables involved in various studies. The categories proposed in this discussion include encoding, decoding, and interactive strategies.

There are undoubtedly other schemes for organizing nonverbal research, but this one should represent distinct approaches fairly well.

Encoding Strategy

In formal communication theory, an idea is encoded into some communication system (sign language, Morse code, speech, etc.), transmitted, received, decoded, and understood. We shall use the term more loosely here to refer to research which focuses on the observation of nonverbal behavior that has been produced in response to specific stimulus conditions. Usually, the stimulus conditions are manipulated by the experimenter so that inferences about causality can be clearly drawn, but one could also employ an encoding strategy in a correlational design. For example, an encoding approach may involve the filmed presentation of specific stimuli, such as a pleasant scene, so that nonverbal reactions to it may be observed. That is, the subject, in observing a particular scene encodes or represents his or her reaction to the scene. This encoding may take place spontaneously, or in some cases it may be deliberate, as, for example, a response to the request, "Show how you would feel or look if this happened to you." Encoding variations may also be the product of verbal instructions, which, like a filmed presentation, can be subtle and indirect or a direct request for a posed or role-played response. Consequently, the primary concern in an encoding strategy involves determining how some process, relationship, or attitude is represented nonverbally by the individual. A current important area of research which frequently employs an encoding strategy is the inquiry into the patterns of facial expression resulting from differing emotional states. Discussion of some of this research is included in the chapters on emotion and individual differences.

Some researchers favor an encoding approach for studying nonverbal communication because they feel that communication requires some intention or purpose on the part of the actor when relating to another person (Ekman & Friesen, 1969; MacKay, 1972). Thus, according to this interpretation of nonverbal communication, the sender or actor must intend to transmit a "message" by, or have a purpose in, his or her nonverbal behavior. Given this interpretation, the only way one can be relatively certain that a particular set of behaviors is designed to communicate is by directly asking or facilitating the sender's nonverbal attitude or reaction, that is, by employing an encoding strategy.

Decoding Strategy

A decoding strategy may be viewed as the opposite of encoding. The focus here is on interpreting the meaning of an actor's nonverbal behavior. While the encoding approach involves the manipulation or selection of various antecedent factors which might influence nonverbal behavior, for example, a fear-arousing movie, the decoding approach involves interpreting, evaluating, or reacting to different patterns of nonverbal behavior, for example, judging facial expressions.[1] In an encoding strategy, nonverbal behaviors are the dependent variables, but in a decoding strategy they are the independent variables. Obviously a decoding strategy can be used to examine the same issues as an encoding strategy, but the focus of the problem is switched from the subject as actor or initiator to the subject as reactor, or even as judge or rater of another's nonverbal behavior. Another contrast between encoding and decoding strategies is that an encoding strategy is typically very reactive in the sense that subjects usually know they are in a study. In contrast, a decoding strategy may be designed so that subjects are not aware that they are participating in a study. For example, violations of norms regarding nonverbal intimacy may be manipulated by a confederate in a field setting, and the subjects' reactions monitored, without their awareness.

Occasionally a decoding approach is used to determine the meaning or interpretation that subjects give to specific patterns of nonverbal behavior between other individuals. Thus, rather than participating in an interaction, they may observe others interact and make judgments of degree of liking or relationship, type of emotions expressed, or perhaps even the content of an unheard conversation. This particular technique can be effectively used with film or videotape tech-

---

[1] A good example of contrasting encoding and decoding strategies can be found in a study by Mehrabian (1968c) which examines the relationship between patterns of nonverbal behavior and attitudes toward another person.

niques, which insure the constancy of the conditions over time and provide easy viewing for large numbers of subjects.

Interactive Strategy

An interactive strategy focuses on the examination of the non-verbal exchanges between individuals. Consequently, the relevant behaviors are studied sequentially as they develop in a social encounter. Usually this assumes that each person's behavior is free to vary as a function of the other's behavior. In the case of confederate–subject interactions, the confederate's behavior should be contingent to some degree on the subject's reaction. For example, experiments which examine the effects of norm violations with constant confederate patterns of intrusion or staring probably should not be categorized as an interactive strategy, but rather as a decoding one; that is, the subject has to interpret and react to the confederate's behavior, but there is no real exchange involved.

An interactive strategy is usually adopted when a researcher wants to study patterns of sequential change in nonverbal behavior. A good example of this approach is Duncan's (1972) study of the cues involved in turn taking in conversations. Duncan's observations and analysis essentially identified sequential probabilities between the occurrence of certain behaviors such as relaxing gestures, gaze behavior, and increases in pause length and the occurrence of a switch in listener–speaker roles. An interactive strategy may also be employed when the effects of individual, relationship, or situational differences are examined. Again, however, the emphasis is on the developing exchange process and not just on a simple immediate reaction such as a facial expression or an avoidance behavior.

RESPONSE MEASURES

The selection of appropriate response measures is determined not only by the substance of a research question but also by concerns about validity, ethics, and strategy. Once an investigator begins with a specific problem or interest, early planning decisions are likely to affect the options available at a number of different levels. For example, if a researcher decides, for good reason, that control of problems relating to the influences of extraneous variables is paramount for a particular problem, then that researcher is more likely to plan an experimental study in a laboratory setting. That decision, in turn, has implications for ethics, strategy, and other aspects of validity. In this case, external validity (generalizability) may suffer somewhat in the laboratory setting, but the mechanics of managing the ethical guidelines will be simpler. In addition, any one of the three strategies outlined here may be easily implemented in a laboratory setting. Finally, and most relevant for the present discussion, the variety and precision of dependent measures is considerably increased in the laboratory. In this example it may seem that the advantages of the laboratory clearly outweigh the disadvantages, but the importance of external validity, especially in attempting to apply the results to real-world settings (e.g., nonverbal exchange between an employer and an employee) should not be underestimated. Keeping in mind that these various decisions are interdependent, let us examine briefly some of the options available among dependent measures.

Measurement Options

Most of the commonly used measures available for researching nonverbal behavior can be identified as falling into one of the following categories: (1) nonverbal behavior measures, (2) physiological measures, (3) ratings, (4) surveys, (5) simulations, and (6) task performance. In many studies, two or more different types of measures are used. This provides an opportunity for testing a hypothesis more extensively by examining the potential convergence of different measures. The following description of these measures and the circumstances under which they may be employed should provide some grasp of their application.

Nonverbal measures cover a wide range of behaviors, including facial expression, visual behavior, gestures, postures, movements, and various paralinguistic cues, among others. Nonverbal behaviors are most frequently used as dependent measures in studies employing encoding or interactive strategies. In decoding studies, nonverbal measures are employed as independent variables, but they may also be used as dependent measures in the same studies. Whether the behavioral measures are observed live, filmed, or videotaped, some observer judgment is almost always required.[2] When observers are required to make a quantitative or qualitative judgment of some behavior, it is critical that such judgments be reliable. In practice, this means that different raters should be able to make comparable judgments about specific instances of behavior. Some index of interrater reliability is usually reported preliminary to the analysis of the behavioral data. In general, the measurement of multiple nonverbal behaviors is most desirable. Usually the researcher will have a better understanding of the subject's overall reaction by observing several related behaviors. For example, there is considerable information that the nonverbal intimacy behaviors (distance, eye contact, touch, lean, and smiling) are dynamically related to one another (Patterson, 1973b, 1976). Consequently, interpreting the meaning or impact of any single intimacy behavior in an interaction is possible only if one knows how the other intimacy behaviors were simultaneously used.

Physiological measures are infrequently employed in nonverbal research, but there is a developing interest in the role of physiological arousal in both nonverbal intimacy and emotional expressiveness. For these and other issues, the measurement of various indicators of arousal becomes a central concern. Electrodermal responses, heart rate, and electroencephalogram (EEG) responses are among the most commonly used physiological measures. Because these measures require rather elaborate, sophisticated instrumentation, the subject is necessarily aware of the procedure. In addition, such measurement almost always requires a controlled laboratory setting to insure that the physiological readings are free of artifacts. Some progress has been made in the use of telemetric monitoring of various physiological changes (the person can move about freely while body readings are transmitted to a remote receiver), but such techniques are usually much more vulnerable to various sources of interference than are their more restrictive counterparts.

Ratings, focusing on self-reactions, impressions of others, and evaluations of settings, experiences, or activities, constitute the most

---

[2] For some measures, particularly paralinguistic cues, completely automated scoring systems could analyze voice tracks for duration of speaking and silence periods, loudness, and component frequencies, and have the record printed out without the need for a human observer.

commonly used measures in psychological research. However, in encoding and interactive strategies, ratings are not usually the primary measures used but are important supplementary sources of data. Of course, when nonverbal behaviors are manipulated in decoding studies, ratings of personal reactions or judgments of others are of central importance. Interpreting data patterns from one or more of the other measures can be more confidently undertaken when rating data converge on a particular explanation. Obviously, self-ratings, like the physiological measures, cannot be employed without the subject's awareness of participation in that effort. However, the true purpose of the ratings may be disguised in an attempt to minimize response bias or demand characteristics of the setting. Finally, observer ratings may be used effectively in any kind of setting, with any kind of design and problem.

Survey data, like self-rating data, constitute a type of self-report information. A survey may contain ratings, but the focus of a survey is likely to be broader and deeper in scope than a set of ratings. The issues pursued in a survey format are usually correlational in nature. That is, the researcher will be concerned with the presence of patterns of relationships among variables, as reported by the subject. For example, subjects might be asked a number of questions relating to their nonverbal interaction patterns with different people in various public settings. In addition, specific nonverbal reactions might be examined with respect to a variety of background or demographic characteristics. Inferences about causality are very risky, but the presence of specific relationships may direct the researcher to further studies, which may identify causal links more clearly. Because of the ease of collecting a considerable amount of information quickly, surveys are very useful measures, particularly early in the development of a research problem.

Simulation techniques involve representational approximations of social settings which permit subjects to indicate how they would behave in an actual setting. Simulation measures seem to be used exclusively with behaviors of distance and orientation. In fact, Altman (1975) found that before 1973 more simulation studies of distance were reported than either laboratory or field studies. A commonly used technique is Kuethe's (1962) social schemata task, which involves the placement of cutouts of human figures on some neutral background. This technique might be used to examine the different grouping patterns or distances employed as a function of the represented characteristics of the figures (e.g., sex, race, age) or to test the influence of different instructions or settings on figure placements. In addition, one might also compare differences on this task as a function of individual differences in the subjects. While this technique has considerable appeal because of its simplicity and ease in collecting data, there are doubts about the value of such measures. Mixed results regarding the relationships between various representational measures, including these figure placement tasks, and behavioral measures of interaction distance bring into question the external validity of simulation studies. Our orientation throughout this book reflects this skepticism by emphasizing behavioral measures over simulation measures.

The last general category of measures, *performance on various tasks or activities*, represents a more indirect way of assessing the influence of nonverbal behavior in social settings. Performance of many kinds of tasks is often influenced by states of arousal, stress, or anxiety. Consequently, some manipulations of nonverbal behavior, which are capable of producing arousal or stress, can be indirectly assessed by observing performance levels on different tasks. For example, if performance on a complicated cognitive activity, such as solving difficult anagrams, is negatively influenced by stress, and scores decrease under conditions of high intimacy, then there is indirect evidence that high intimacy produces stress. Of course, alternative hypotheses may have to be weighed, including, in this particular example, simple distraction. However, performance measures are often useful when more direct measures are impractical for some reason. When performance measures are used, it is desirable to increase confidence in the inferences that may be drawn. Occasionally a researcher may have applied interests which are specifically focused on some performance measure. In that case, understanding performance patterns becomes an end in itself, and not a means to the end of inferring something about arousal or stress.

In concluding this section, there are a few points which seem worthy of emphasis. First, decisions at different levels of planning research have distinct implications for the options available at other levels. While it may be simple to think of the planning process as a sequential one moving from general to specific considerations, particular concerns or problems at a specific level may sequentially precede more general decisions. Second, we have attempted to balance some of the traditional emphasis on internal validity in planning research by discussing a number of more subtle limitations posed by external validity and ethical considerations. Finally, a careful and deliberate assessment of measurement options is critical, and attempts should be made to employ multiple measures of the process under investigation.

A CASE STUDY: WALKING INTRUSIONS

Even lucid, uncomplicated discussions of design and methodology can be difficult to appreciate fully without the use of examples. What we will attempt to do here is to apply the issues discussed earlier to a specific study conducted by one of the authors. It would be tempting to say that this study has been selected because of its excellent methodology, unambiguous results, and profound impact on nonverbal research—tempting, but unfortunately not true. However, the mix of strong and weak points in this study may provide a good vehicle for applying the earlier discussion. This particular study was entitled "Walking Intrusions: Proximity for a Change of Pace" (Patterson, Kelly, & Douglas, 1977).

Background

The specific impetus for this study developed out of an interest in the role of arousal in precipitating nonverbal adjustments to inappropriately high intimacy. Substantial evidence has been found showing that inappropriately high intimacy initiated by one person frequently produces behavioral adjustments by the other to reduce that intimacy (Patterson, 1973b). A typical instance of this adjustment might involve one's turning or leaning away and possibly avoiding eye contact in response to a stranger's close approach. Furthermore, results from laboratory studies indicate that close approaches by an experimenter can produce increases in arousal (Gale, Spratt, Chapman, & Smallbone, 1975; McBride, King & James, 1965). One theoretical explanation for the sequence of adjustment reactions is that substantial increases in intimacy precipitate arousal which mediates the type of behavioral adjustment made (Patterson, 1976). More specifically, arousal which is experienced negatively (fear or anxiety) will lead to behavioral attempts to decrease the intimacy of the other, while arousal which is experienced positively (liking or love) will lead to attempts to increase intimacy. A complete discussion of this model is covered in chapter 5.

The most direct test of the mediating role of arousal would, of course, involve measuring arousal change in response to variations in intimacy. Frankly, at the time that we started the study we lacked both the instrumentation and expertise necessary to conduct such an experiment in the laboratory. Consequently, we focused on a less direct tack by using a field setting and inferring potential arousal from ratings and behavioral measures. The obvious disadvantages of this alternative were the inability to measure arousal directly and the reduced control of the field setting—both constraints on internal validity. The major advantage was the increased external validity possible by gathering data in natural settings from a slightly more heterogeneous group of subjects.

Design and Procedure

A common way in which intimacy is manipulated in field settings is through the use of spatial intrusions—inappropriately close approaches—to a naive seated subject by a confederate of the experimenter. We searched for a new wrinkle on this technique, while still manipulating distance, and came up with the idea of structuring a walking spatial intrusion. Basically this consisted of the confederate maintaining a side-by-side distance of approximately 1 foot from the subject as he or she walked down a stretch of sidewalk. Our hypothesis was that such an intrusion should produce an adjustive response, such as speeding up to lose the intruder, and that self-ratings by the subject might reflect a corresponding change in affect. From changes both in rated affect and behavioral adjustments one might make a tentative inference regarding increased arousal. Again, although this design does not permit the clean interpretations that might be made by directly measuring arousal in the laboratory, it does provide suggestive evidence, with some increase in external validity compared to a laboratory study. Because the responses to the intrusion might vary as a function of sex of the subject and sex of the intruder, those factors were included in the design. Finally male and female control groups, experiencing no intrusion, were necessary for comparison purposes. Thus there were four experimental and two control conditions in the study. This design would be classified as a decoding strategy because the nonverbal behavior was manipulated and the consequences were measured on behavioral and rating scales.

The experiment required three assistants, including the intruder, the observer-rater, and the interviewer who approached for the affect ratings. A location was chosen where there was a long, flat, straight stretch of sidewalk on campus. A distance of 170 feet was marked as the intrusion zone by a tree on one end and a trash can on the other. The intruder was positioned off to the side so that the approaching subject would not easily see him or her. The observer was seated on the ground near the start of the 170-foot zone, while the interviewer was just beyond the end of that zone. The experiment was conducted during afternoon hours, sufficiently outside of class change times so that only a small number of people were on the sidewalk at any time. The observer signaled a subject's approach to the intruder so that the intruder could begin walking and be in phase with the subject at the start of the intrusion zone. The intruder attempted to maintain side-by-side position for the full length of the intrusion zone and walked away only at its ending point. As soon as the intruder changed direction, the interviewer approached the subject with the rating material.

Dependent Measures

A variety of dependent measures were assessed in this study. First, walking speed was recorded by the observer who inconspicuously timed the duration it took the subject to cover the 170-foot zone. Second, a number of behavioral ratings were made by the observer for the first 48 feet of the intrusion zone (marked by a light post), which was a distance over which the observer could see the subject clearly enough to make judgments of various behavioral adjustments. These observations included judgments of directional gaze, movement toward or away from the intruder, and the presence or absence of scratching. The last measure was included as a specific behavioral index of arousal (see Chapman, 1975; Kleck, 1970). The interrater reliability on nine estimates of walking by two different judges was $r = +.94$. For the behavioral ratings, there was agreement on 42 of 45 judgments (9 subjects × 5 behaviors) between two raters. However, some caution is needed in interpreting this apparently high level of agreement because of the low rate of these behaviors. For the nine subjects there were only five instances in which either rater judged any of the behaviors present and there was disagreement in three of those cases. Finally, the self-ratings of affect included 7-point scales of nine bipolar adjectives such as pleasant-unpleasant, bad-good, excited-calm.

When the interviewer approached the subject, he or she told the subject that the purpose of the ratings was to determine the effect of time of day, temperature, and weather conditions on mood states. The true purpose of the ratings was disguised because we wanted to maintain our cover for the intrusion manipulation and not risk the chance of the study being known to later subjects. It is interesting to note that although a few subjects were amused by our apparent concern with the time, temperature, and weather, no one expressed any suspicion of a link between the immediately preceding intrusion and the request for the ratings.

Ethics

The first ethical concern with the procedure outlined here is that subjects' consent could not be sought without informing them of what to expect. However, there would be little sense in attempting the manipulation if consent was sought first and the subject was prepared for what followed. A second issue involves the potential harm to the subject. In this case, it is assumed that whatever little discomfort arises from the intruder's presence should be slight and short-term. Later data from the ratings did support this assumption. Maintenance of anonymity of the subject's data was no problem because no one knew any of the subjects and names were not requested on the rating forms. A simple number and condition code identified various pieces of data. Deception was employed in the interviewer's cover for the purpose of the ratings, but it is difficult to see how that could adversely affect the subject. Before we could begin collecting data, a campus committee on human subjects evaluated and approved our proposed treatment of subjects.

Results

The results of the study showed mixed support for the hypothesized role of arousal in mediating behavioral adjustments to inappropriate intimacy. The effect of the confederate's paced intrusion can be seen in Table 1. Although none of the four intrusion means differed significantly from the controls, differences were found between intrusion conditions. Intruded males walked significantly faster than intruded females, independent of the sex of the intruder. It is interesting to note that the walking speeds of male and female control subjects were essentially identical and fell between the means of the male and female intrusion subjects. Some marginal evidence for the presence of arousal during the intrusion was found in the behavioral measure of scratching. Specifically, 8 of 32 intrusion subjects scratched at least once, while none of the 16 control subjects did. An analysis of the mood ratings showed no significant effects of the intrusion manipulation.

Evaluating the Evidence

The results did show that the manner of adjusting to the intrusions differed as a function of the sex of the subject. Furthermore, there was some indirect evidence, in the form of intruded subjects scratching more than controls, that the intrusion produced arousal.

Table 1. Mean Walking Pace through Intrusion Zone (ft/sec)[a]

	Intruder Sex		
Subject Sex	Male	Female	Control
Male	5.02a	5.13a	4.79ab
Female	4.34b	4.24b	4.80ab

[a] Means not sharing a common subscript differ significantly from one another at the .05 level by the Newman-Kuels test.

However, even this marginal effect is questionable because of the failure to demonstrate clearly an adequate level of interrater reliability. Finally, the absence of any intrusion effects on the mood ratings presents the greatest difficulty for the arousal mediation hypothesis. Nevertheless, it is still possible that the intrusion did cause arousal and its accompanying change in mood state, but it was not registered in the ratings. Specifically, the 10 or 15 seconds between the end of the intrusion and the start of the ratings may be long enough to produce an elation effect. That is, the mood of the intruded subjects may reflect relief at having "lost" the intruder, making their ratings comparable to the controls, even though their mood was more negative during the intrusion. Such a possibility, while reasonable, does not take the place of clearly supportive results.

Future Prospects

The results of this research endeavor are not clear enough by themselves to represent a direct advance in our understanding of the role of arousal in nonverbal adjustments. Such a conclusion is not just a rare instance of modesty on our part, but also the convergent judgment of reviewers from two different journals who passed up an opportunity to publish our manuscript. However, our pursuit of truth, or a reasonable approximation thereof, is not easily stunted. We have recently completed a laboratory study in which nonverbal intimacy was manipulated and both physiological and behavioral measures were simultaneously observed. This latter study gives us a more direct and controlled test of the arousal mediation hypothesis, while sacrificing some external validity. The results of that study show some modest support for the arousal mediation hypothesis (Patterson, Jordan, Hogan, & Frerker, 1981).

We are also planning another walking intrusion study which (we hope) will resolve some of the procedural difficulties of the first study. Instead of using the rating measures, we hope to film, or at least photograph, the subjects' behaviors during the intrusion manipulation. This will permit us to have a permanent record of the subjects' reactions which can be rated later by judges who are naive about the purpose and design of the study—a control we were not able to institute in the first study. In addition we can use facial expressions as a reliable index of degree of positive or negative affect during the intrusions. If changes in this latter measure can be related to other behavioral reactions, one could have a clearer interpretation of the sequential developments over time.

Gradually, by refining our techniques, filling in gaps, and paying attention to the nagging inconsistencies in our results, our efforts should bring us closer to understanding these processes. It is rare that a single study resolves an issue, so we as researchers must be prepared to follow our best leads from one study to the next. In doing so, we may generate as many questions as answers, but that, too, is a desirable end of research.

CHAPTER 2

Nonverbal Aspects of Attraction

"You could have been so high and mighty in this world, that when you looked down on the plain, dumb, ordinary people of poor old Rosewater County, we would look like bugs."

"Now, now—"

"You gave up everything a man is supposed to want, just to help the little people, and the little people know it. God bless you, Mr. Rosewater. Good night."

Why do some people like other people? Vonnegut's (1965, p. 74) Elliott Rosewater was liked because of his goodness and helpfulness. Other people are liked for different reasons, the major ones being that they (1) satisfy some need of the person who likes them, (2) they are similar to that person, (3) they are desirable or attractive, or (4) they are close at hand. Before we discuss the role of nonverbal behavior, we will first summarize major conclusions from attraction research, as collected into these four categories.

FACTORS THAT CONTRIBUTE TO ATTRACTION

Reinforcement

According to Thibaut and Kelley (1959), social reinforcements act as an implicit medium of exchange in interpersonal relations. They propose that people choose to spend time with other people because the other people are more pleasant or reinforcing than are the available alternatives. Homans (1961) has also proposed an "economic man" model of social relations: if a person considers that the rewards are not proportional to the costs in a relationship, he or she will feel angry and resent the other person. Thus we are attracted toward those who treat us fairly, and we try to reciprocate the liking they demonstrate for us in their behavior.

Similarity

Some of the dimensions on which we can be similar to other people are attitudes, appearance, intelligence, personality, and social characteristics. Similarity in attitudes has received the most testing and theoretical discussion. According to cognitive balance theory (Heider, 1958), we are uncomfortable when our friends do not share our attitudes or when our enemies do. Similarly, according to social comparison theory (Festinger, 1954), it is reinforcing to have others agree with us and punishing to have them disagree with us. If people disagree with us it raises the possibility that we are stupid, immoral, uninformed, or insane.

Whatever the underlying dynamics and motivations, substantial evidence has accumulated showing that increased perceived similarity in attitudes leads to the increased liking of another person (cf. Byrne & Griffitt, 1966; Byrne, Baskett, & Hodges, 1971; Worchel & Mc-Cormick, 1963).

Not only is similarity in attitudes a potential determinant of liking, there is also some evidence that similarity in physical attractiveness leads to some degree of pair bonding. The similarity in attractiveness for couples can be represented by the correlation between the attractiveness scores each gets when rated by judges: the more similar in attractiveness, the higher the correlation. Researchers have found that correlations of objectively rated physical attractiveness of each member of a married couple were $+.72$ in one study, $+.60$ in another, and $+.63$ in a third. Correlations for dating couples were positive but much weaker: $r = +.19$ and $+.18$ in two different studies. Similarity in attractiveness of "serious daters" was $+.56$, greater than mere "dating couples" but not as similar as married couples (Cavior & Boblett, 1972; Murstein, 1972; Murstein & Christy, 1976; White, 1980). White also found that the greater the difference between a couple in attractiveness, the less likely they were to continue dating, and if they did continue, the less likely they were to have progressed to a more serious or intimate relationship. As a side note, we have the finding that even same-sex friends tend to be more similar in objectively rated physical attractiveness than randomly paired groupings (Cash & Derlega, 1978).

Although similarity in intelligence has been found to have little effect on liking in a computer dating setting (Walster, Aronson, Abrahams, & Rottman, 1966), husbands and wives do have similar intelligence scores ($r = +.40$) (Jones, 1929; Reed & Reed, 1965). A major reason for these divergent findings seems to be that computer and blind dates place a premium on first-impression characteristics such as attractiveness, thus lessening the potential influence of intelligence. In addition, within the population most likely to use computer dating, the range of intelligence is small, which necessarily limits the potential relationship between intelligence and attraction.

In general, the relationship between attraction and similarity of personality is weak. However, it is not as weak as the antithetical notion that opposites attract, dominant people seek out submissive partners, and nurturant and dependent people seek out each other, either consciously or unconsciously (Izard, 1960; 1963).

A study by Reiss (1965) indicates that attraction is increased by similarity in social status. He found that the selection of serious dating partners tended to be from the fraternity or sorority whose social status was similar to one's own. This tendency of people to associate with others of like socioeconomic status has been documented a number of times, since the early study of *Elmtown's Youth* (Hollingshead, 1949).

It appears that similarity in race and religion substantially influence potential attraction. As Rubin (1973) put it:

> According to 1960 Census data, whites in the United States surpass Ivory Snow by being 99.8 percent pure, with only one-fifth of 1 percent marrying nonwhites. Similarly, 99 percent of black Americans marry fellow blacks.

Probably for the same reasons, Americans married someone of the same religion in 93.6% of the cases in 1957. It seems very likely that these figures would have changed considerably over the last 20 or 25 years, but the race and religion are undoubtedly still important factors in attraction. Furthermore, it should be kept in mind that the above figures are based on self-report data given by married people. As such, they probably represent some inflation in the apparent level of homogamy because people may have changed their definition of their race to that of their spouse, or converted to their spouse's religion. Sometimes the two shift to a third religion or to no religion.

We have seen how liking is affected by similarity in appearance, attitudes, and other attributes, such as intelligence, personality, and social characteristics. However, it would be oversimplifying matters to say that it was the similarity that necessarily *caused* the selection of friend or spouse. We shall consider an alternative viewpoint in the next section.

Desirability and Attractiveness

In the last section we focused on similarity between people as a determinant of their liking for one another. A moment's reflection, however, reminds us that there are limits to the similarity-attraction view. We also expect people to be attracted to others who exceed them in beauty and ability. Let us first examine people's reactions to someone who is attractive.

In 1972, Dion, Berscheid, and Walster demonstrated that people associate a number of socially desirable traits with physical attractiveness. The assumption that beauty is associated with goodness has even been generalized to the notion that information conveyed by a more attractive communication source should probably also be more persuasive. Such a communication-source effect has in fact been found (Chaiken, 1979). However, subsequent research found attractiveness had no effect on persuasiveness, despite the study's strong support of the beautiful-is-good finding (Maddux & Rogers, 1980). The physically attractive source was rated as more sociable, interesting, warm, outgoing, poised, strong, sexually warm and responsive, and interpersonally attractive!

As long as people sense that attractiveness is associated in the minds of other people with other positive attributes (and vice versa), people will make those assumed reactions part of their definition of their social situation. In a study by Kleck and Strenta (1980), three groups of subjects were led to believe that a confederate (1) saw a scar on their face, (2) thought they were mildly epileptic, or (3) thought they had a mild allergy. The first two groups felt that the confederate was being strongly influenced by the information or observation, was made tense by it, and viewed the subject as less attractive, in comparison to the third group. Even when a woman has not been stigmatized by a scar or a label such as "epileptic," she has reason to be made uneasy by the overly critical attitude of males in evaluating the attractiveness of women. There is good evidence that such a critical attitude is strengthened by male exposure to standards of beauty that few women can attain, as in *Playboy* magazine or the television show "Charlie's Angels" (Kenrick & Gutierres, 1980).

It would appear that attractiveness influences attraction, although the exact nature and extent of that relationship has still to be defined. Of the many other characteristics that someone can possess, his or her position on a hierarchy of ability should probably influence other people's attraction, especially in a culture such as ours, which emphasizes achievement and status. Women students indicated that a man would be unacceptable to them as a date if he had a low status job, such as janitor or bartender, but highly acceptable if he were a physician, lawyer, or chemist (Van Gorp, Stempfle, & Olson, 1969). There appears to be somewhat more concern for this dimension by women than men. Women in one study actually rated ability as important as attractiveness when specifying what was important for a desirable cross-sex relationship. Men rated attractiveness as more important (Coombs & Kenkel, 1966).

It seems possible that the concern for ability and status evidenced by women may be reflecting what they feel they should consider and what their parents told them they should do, because when women rated the success of their blind date and their desire to date their partner again, physical attractiveness was the major determinant, and ability had no influence at all (Walster, Aronson, Abrahams, & Rottmann, 1966). A similar finding was obtained in a later study. Reis, Nezlek, and Wheeler (1980) found that physical attractiveness had more of an impact on the number of social experiences reported by males than by females. However, we still assume that physical attractiveness is probably more important in the early stages of dating but would expect that other characteristics come into play later on in a relationship, such as considerateness (Levinger & Snoek, 1972).

Propinquity

George Homans (1950) amusingly described the impact of propinquity on attraction: "You can get to like some pretty queer customers if you go around with them long enough" (p. 115). He stated
the same point more formally in the same volume: "If the frequency
of interaction between two or more people increases, their degree of
liking for one another increases" (p. 112).

Propinquity is not just a determinant of attraction but also an
intensifier of involvement, both positive and negative. First of all,
there is Bossard's law—the finding that one-third of the marriage
licenses in a large city are between people who live within five blocks
of each other (Bossard, 1932). If we take the propinquity measure
from where a person grew up, then modern mobility has probably
weakened Bossard's Law. But if we measure propinquity from where
two people are living when they meet, then the law probably holds
up as well or almost as well as it did when formulated. Even though
Bruce is 150 miles from home and falls in love with Sarah who is from
a town that is 400 miles from his hometown, Sarah's sorority is a
block and a half from Bruce's fraternity. In terms of where the person
is living at the time, propinquity begets romantic involvement.

However, there is a less pleasant side to the effect of propinquity
on involvement. We have all heard that "most aggravated assaults
occur within the family unit or among neighbors and acquaintances."
In 1969 the National Commission on the Causes and Prevention of
Violence had this to say about violent crime:

> *Unlike robbery, the other violent crimes of homicide, assault and rape tend to be*
> *acts of passion among intimates and acquaintances.*
> The Victim-Offender Survey shows that homicide and assault usually
> occur between relatives, friends, or acquaintances (about two-thirds to
> three-fourths of the cases in which the relationship is known). They occur
> in the home or other indoor locations about 50–60 percent of the time.
> Rape is more likely to be perpetrated by a stranger (slightly over half of
> the cases), usually in the home or other indoor location (about two-thirds
> of the time). By contrast, robbery is usually committed outside (two-thirds
> of the cases) by a stranger (more than 80 percent of the cases). (pp. 43–44)

Probably homicide, assault, and rape are *all* crimes that are carried
out predominantly among intimates, if we consider that rape is more
likely to go unreported than homicide and assault. In fact, it was not

until 1979 in the highly publicized *Rideout* case that it became possible for a husband to be tried for raping his wife.

Conclusions

It would appear that one determinant of whether two people end up spending time together is initially influenced by propinquity followed temporarily by attractiveness in terms of looks and status, with such other factors as personality playing a role later on in the relationship. But during the phase after propinquity has had its influence and when social attractiveness is a major factor, there seems to be a marketplace interchange involved, where people try to get the best deal they can but usually end up settling for associates who are close to their social value.

The marketplace model of attraction may not ring true to the average person because it seems so cold and unemotional. However, it operates in subtle ways even in the behavior of people who feel that they are motivated by love and friendship only. We associate with people having social values similar to our own through a variety of screening devices such as the cost of homes in a neighborhood, membership requirements in country clubs, fraternities, sororities, and other organizations, and admission requirements to colleges and graduate schools. One can therefore attend to the nonmarketplace characteristics of one's lover because of the institutional and economic prescreening.

If the reader wishes to pursue the topic of attraction, there are a number of useful overviews of the area. Huston's (1974) *Foundations of Interpersonal Attraction;* Berscheid and Walster's (1978) *Interpersonal Attraction;* Clore's (1975) *Interpersonal Attraction: An Overview;* and Duck's (1977) *Theory and Practice in Interpersonal Attraction* should prove helpful.

NONVERBAL BEHAVIOR AND ATTRACTION

We now turn to the major issue addressed by this book: The role of nonverbal behavior in those phenomena that have been studied in the area of social psychology. Attraction would seem to be an especially fruitful area for examining patterns of nonverbal behavior. The nonverbal behaviors with the most promise are interpersonal distance, gazing, smiling, touching, and vocal delivery.

Distance

Response to Distance. As we saw earlier, people claim as their friends, date, marry, beat up, and murder those who live or work close to them; the likelihood of emotional involvement increases as distance decreases. Does the same relationship hold for closer interpersonal distance as it does for city blocks? How do we react when another person stands close to us?

The effect of the kind of interpersonal distance we measure in feet seems to be as complex as the kind we measure in miles. For example, in one study subjects conversed with three confederates, one at a time, who sat at distances of 2, 4, and 8 feet (Porter, Argyle, & Salter, 1970). After each conversation the subjects made 21 ratings of the confederates on such traits as introverted versus extraverted, self-conscious versus at ease, and slow versus fast. Surprisingly, distance had no effect on any of the ratings. That was not the case in another similar study over comparable distances. This time confederates were viewed most favorably at the 4-foot distance, somewhat less favorably at 2 and 6 feet, and least favorably at 8 feet (Patterson, Mullens, & Romano, 1971).

When affective reactions *are* obtained in response to close approaches (spatial invasions), the feelings are usually negative rather than positive (Patterson, 1976). The negative response is thought by some to be due to the violation of norms concerning the appropriate distance for strangers (Garfinkle, 1964). However one wants to conceptualize the reasons, the negative reaction seems to be lawful in terms of conflict theory (Knowles, 1980), that is, people respond as if there are no approach tendencies, merely increasing their avoidance tendencies as the invader gets closer.

Spatial invasion from a stranger has been a continuing interest in the study of interpersonal distance. One question that has been posed is whether some kinds of invasion are more noxious than others. Fisher and Byrne (1975) investigated how students respond when another student casually sits near them at a large rectangular library table. They found that females tended to react negatively if anyone sat on the same side of the table as them (whether it was another woman or a man, and whether it was right next to them or one chair removed). On the other hand, males responded more negatively when someone sat across from them.

As a check on this interaction of sex of subject and type of spatial invasion, Fisher and Byrne sent an observer through the library to note where students sitting alone at tables placed their books and personal effects. Males more often erected barriers across from them and females more often erected adjacent barriers. Thus, women and men in this study differed in what seemed most intrusive to them, but they showed a similar use of blocking techniques to protect themselves.

The majority of the studies in this area indicate that decreased distance creates not attraction but discomfort. Unfortunately, it is also true that the majority of studies have involved spatial invasion by a stranger, rather than by someone who is familiar and intimate with the person. The use of strangers is unfortunate because there is evidence that interpersonal relationship is a strong determinant of nonverbal intimacy (Heslin & Boss, 1980, see chapter 4).

Most of the evidence relating attraction to distance has been focused on relatively close approaches. While the question of attraction has not been directly addressed, there is some information that greater distances, like closer distances, are more uncomfortable than moderate ones (Patterson, 1977; Thompson, Aiello, & Epstein, 1979).

There have been a number of attempts to make sense of the variety of reactions that people have to the distance another person stands or sits from them. Sundstrom and Altman (1976) proposed that there are four variables affecting a person's response to another person's close approach: (1) the social and personal relationship between the two people involved (whether they know and like each other); (2) their expectation of interaction; (3) the intimacy of the topic of conversation; and (4) the physical constraints of the situation, for example, noise level.

Sundstrom and Altman designated three basic kinds of situations that have different dynamics and prognoses of how people react to closeness: (1) a person is talking to a friend or relative, (2) a person is talking to a stranger or casual acquaintance, and (3) a person sees a stranger and does not want to talk to him or her. They point out that most of the early discussions of interpersonal distance did not differentiate among these three kinds of situations. Figure 1 depicts the predicted degree of comfort a person should experience as a function of the situation and the distance from the other person.

Note that there is a saddle point of optimal distance when a given interaction (among friends or strangers) is occurring. That is, it is unpleasant to try to talk to someone who is either too far away or too close. The third situation, the one involving strangers without interaction, has no optimum distance or saddle point. The farther away the stranger, the more comfortable it is for the person. One common prediction that was made for all three situations was that closeness would be viewed with discomfort. Such a prediction is at variance with any notion that intimacy begets intimacy.

Patterson (1976) proposed a somewhat different approach, which might help to make sense of the discrepant findings on interpersonal distance and other nonverbal behaviors. Basically, Patterson's model proposes that the response to changes in another's interaction distance (or gaze, touch, etc.) is mediated by the emotional reaction to that approach. In the simplest case, if there is no change in affect or emotion, then there will similarly be no adjustment reaction required to the change in distance. However, if the emotional reaction is a positively labeled one (e.g., liking, love), then the response will be one of reciprocating the increased proximity of the other person.

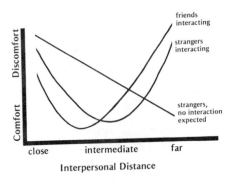

Figure 1. A theoretical model of personal space as a function of interpersonal relationship and expectation of interaction. (From "Interpersonal relationships and personal space: Research review and theoretical model" by E. Sundstrom & I. Altman, *Human Ecology*, 1976, 4, 47–67. Redrawn by Knowles, 1980. Reprinted by permission.)

Consequently, one might smile, lean forward, touch, or hug the other and feel increased attraction. In contrast, a negative emotional reaction (e.g., fear, anxiety) would facilitate a compensatory adjustment to the other person's increased proximity. Such a response might involve turning or leaning away from the other person and generally feeling more negative toward him or her—a response pattern typical in most spatial-invasion studies. A more complete description of this model can be found in chapter 5.

A third approach which attempts to explain the diverse results on interaction distance has been proposed by Knowles (1980). He analyzes in detail Argyle and Dean's (1965) assumption that the interpersonal equilibrium in intimacy reflects the approach–avoidance conflict described by N. E. Miller (1944). (See chapter 5 for a more detailed presentation of equilibrium theory.) The basic description of this conflict is that people simultaneously experience both a desire to move closer to others and a desire to stay away from them. For example, this might involve the contrasting needs for privacy versus intimacy. Miller had originally proposed that the drive to approach gets stronger the closer an organism gets to its goal. This is in keeping with a model tested on rats, which uses food pellets in a goal box to assess the approach gradient. Knowles believes that interpersonal approach forces are similar to people's approach pattern to a potbellied stove on a cold day. When a person is very cold (far from the stove), the desire to approach the stove is very strong. When the person is close and quite warm, the desire to approach closer is low. Thus, instead of motivation to approach becoming stronger the closer one gets, as in Miller's model and Hull's (1932) "goal gradient," the motivation to approach becomes weaker the closer one gets to the other person.

Knowles is in agreement with Sundstrom and Altman (1976) that a distinction has to be made between interaction and noninteraction situations. In his terms, the main characteristic of the noninteraction encounter with a stranger (he or she simply moves close) is an absence of an approach gradient or desire to move closer to the other person at any distance. Given that the avoidance gradient is greater the closer the other person is, then the resultant force will be one of avoidance that is stronger at very close distances and weaker at far distances (see Figure 2A and 2B).

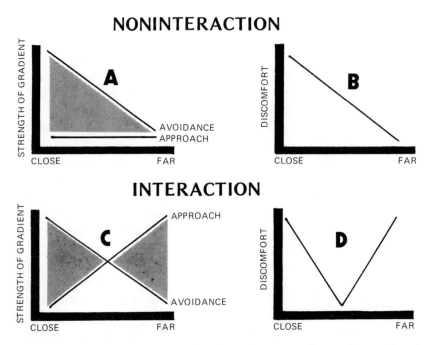

Figure 2. Approach–avoidance conflict theory showing gradients of approach and avoidance and resultant discomfort. (From "An affiliative-conflict theory of personal and group spatial behavior" by E. S. Knowles, 1980. Reprinted by permission.)

If the two people are talking or going to talk, however, then both approach and avoidance tendencies come into play (see Figure 2C and 2D). Some point will result where the two tendencies are equal and where there is greatest comfort. Thus if two friends are conversing and the chairs in the room are at a distance beyond the interaction point of one of the person's approach and avoidance gradient, he or she will manifest discomfort with the distance by such things as sitting forward in his or her chair, leaning forward, looking intently at the other person, and so on. Although a recent test of the curvilinear model found support for it, the authors did not report any difference between an interaction and a noninteraction setting (Thompson, Aiello, & Epstein, 1979).

It takes an Auden (1976) to capture in a few lines the essence of that which we so laboriously rediscover by empirical means:

Some thirty inches from my nose
The frontier of my Person goes,
And all the untilled air between
Is private *pagus* or demesne.
Stranger, unless with bedroom eyes
I beckon you to fraternize,
Beware of rudely crossing it:
I have no gun, but I can spit.[1]

Spatial Response to Liking. We have already examined the effects of differing approach distances on personal reactions and impressions toward others. In most cases, especially between strangers, close approaches produce negative reactions and unfavorable impressions. However, looking at this issue from the contrasting perspective, it is clear that the *choice* of interaction distance may reflect differential degrees of attraction or liking. People stand closer when they are attracted to someone (Evans & Howard, 1973; Gottheil, Corey, & Paredes, 1968; Kleinke, 1972; Mehrabian, 1972); they infer positive feelings when they are shown couples at close interpersonal distance (Guardo, 1969; Kelly, 1972); and they place figures at closer distances when there is greater attraction between the people the figures represent (Guardo, 1969; Little, 1965). Children place themselves at a greater distance from threatening persons both in their actual behavior (King, 1966) and symbolically in placement of silhouettes (Guardo & Meisels, 1971). When college students are insulted they increase the size of their body buffer zone generally, but especially toward the insulter (O'Neal, Brunault, Carifio, Troutwine, & Epstein, 1980). In addition, intimacy of relationship and distance have been found to be inversely related in greeting and saying goodbye at the airport, (Heslin & Boss, 1980, see chapter 4) and in initiating conversation (Heshka & Nelson, 1972; Willis, 1966).

There is some evidence that even though liking leads to closeness, anger can at times also lead to moving close to another person, although in this case it might be called "counterattack by invasion of

---

[1] From "Prologue: The Birth of Architecture" by W. H. Auden. In *W. H. Auden: Collected Poems*, edited by Edward Mendelson. Copyright 1965 by W. H. Auden. Random House, New York. Reprinted by permission.

the other's space," (Meisels & Dosey, 1971). With that exception, we can conclude that people tend to move closer to others they like, and observers infer that a closer distance means that the person likes the other.

Visual Behavior

Pupillary Dilation.   We will first consider in this section a response that is both similar to, yet different from, gazing—pupillary dilation. Pupillary dilation or constriction is a visual behavior, but unlike gaze direction, it is apparently not under conscious control, and changes in dilation are obviously much more subtle behaviors than changes in gaze direction. Nevertheless, pupillary dilation seems to be a very interesting interactive behavior. The pupil has been used as a nonverbal indicator of arousal, dilating when the person views something interesting and attractive, and constricting when the person views something unpleasant (Hess, 1975; Hess & Polt, 1960). It has also been found that people respond more favorably to photographs in which the pupils have been enlarged than those in which they have been made smaller. Perhaps we like others when their pupillary response (dilation) indicates that they like us, that is, if we are able to notice that dilation.

Gazing as an Antecedent of Liking.   One ingenious study compared the relative influence of pupillary dilation and gaze direction on liking of a confederate (Stass & Willis, 1967). Each subject was led to a waiting room and told he would be asked to choose a partner from the other two "subjects" he would meet in the waiting room. The subject was told to pick a partner who would be both pleasant and trustworthy. The confederates were contrasted in terms of amount of gaze directed toward the subject (low versus high gaze) and amount of pupil dilation (produced by use of a drug). The subjects were strongly and positively affected by the gazing of the confederate, but pupillary dilation also had an effect on the choice of a partner. However, the effect of pupil dilation was not nearly as strong as that of gazing. It is also interesting to note that a few of the subjects mentioned eye contact as a factor in their choice, but none of them mentioned the pupillary dilation.

In a more recent study, Wiemann (1974) had his confederates gaze 100%, 75%, 25%, or 0% of the time they were being interviewed.

He found that although interviewees who gaze more at subjects were not seen by them as more dominant, potent, or confident, they were seen as more friendly. The 75% gaze confederates were seen as most friendly and were significantly more likely to be chosen by the subject interviewers. In another study of interviewer behavior, it was also found the male subjects were most unfavorable toward female interviewers who gazed least. Specifically, subjects rated interviewers who looked away as least attentive (especially if they were unattractive), gave them the shortest answers, and sat farthest from them during the debriefing session (Kleinke, Staneski, & Berger, 1975). It appears that the subjects interpreted interviewers' failure to look at them as meaning they did not like the subjects.

Increased gazing toward another may also signal increased involvement that may not necessarily be positive (Ellsworth & Carlsmith, 1968; Goffman, 1963). For example, Ellsworth, Carlsmith, and Henson (1972) demonstrated that a stranger gazing at the driver of a car waiting for a red light to change causes the driver to move through an intersection more rapidly when the light changes than someone who is not the object of a stare. Similarly, Exline (1972), Morris (1967), and others have discussed the power of the gaze to elicit an aggressive response in a recipient. Gallup (1972) demonstrated that tonic immobility in lizards and chickens is induced by gazing, and that the length of the immobility can be markedly shortened by covering the eyes of the hawk. As any marine recruit can attest, there is little in this world so withering as the intense stare of a drill instructor toward one of his hapless leathernecks. Thus we have evidence that different types of gazing can be interpreted as a positive or negative signal.

There is one aspect of gazing that is often overlooked. It is that a distinction should be made between the number of times a person gazes versus the duration of the look. For example, Kendon and Cook (1969) found no relation between liking and the amount of looking but did find that partners were liked more if they used fewer and longer gazes rather than shorter, more frequent ones. The long, intense gaze, then, seems to have the special meaning of high involvement, as we see in these few lines from Gogol's *Dead Souls* (1842/ 1961): "Manilov was touched—beyond words. The two friends clasped hands for a long time, looking mutely into each other's eyes, in which tears were welling."

Gazing as a Consequence of Liking. In general, the evidence seems to indicate that when we like someone we will tend to look at him or her. Generally, people seem to be conscious of this relationship.

In an experiment in which some subjects received negative and others positive evaluations from an interviewer, those who had received a negative evaluation subsequently gazed less at the interviewer (Exline & Winters, 1965). Similarly, it had been found that when people have come to expect social approval from another person (as a result of friendly previous discussion), they will look more at that person than at a person from whom they have no such expectation (Efran & Broughton, 1966).

The predisposition to look more at someone who is liked should be even stronger among lovers than among those who merely like each other very much. In fact, Rubin (1973) has documented such an effect. Rubin contrasted couples whose members mutually indicated strong love for one another with those who indicated a lesser degree of love. The couples scoring higher on Rubin's love scale held mutual gaze longer than those scoring lower. This was apparently not due to some generalized tendency for higher gaze by those who report being strongly in love. When people who scored high on the love scale were paired with strangers who scored high on the scale they did not engage in more mutual gaze than low scorers.

Thus, there is evidence that the more another person is liked the more we gaze at him or her. However it would be an overextension of these limited findings to assume that such a positive relationship occurs all of the time until further research in more varied settings has been conducted. For example, a study found that when males were told that they had looked at a female at a level which was significantly less than usual for most people, they were *more* favorable toward her than males who were told that they had gazed at the female a lot (Kleinke, Bustos, Meeker, & Staneski, 1973). So much for our convenient and invariant generalizations.

Touching

Touching is a form of nonverbal behavior which implies interpersonal involvement, but the tone of the involvement must be determined by the nature of the touch situation. Concentrating on what are usually considered positive touches, it appears that the meaning of a touch can be quite ambiguous. For example, a study by Pattison (1973) found that the counselor's touching did not make clients feel that the counselor was more empathic, warm, or genuine or that the counseling situation was more intense or intimate. Yet, when psychiatric nurses used touch gestures in a hospital setting they had better rapport and received more approach behavior from patients (Aguilera, 1967).

A type of touching that may be considered pleasant by one segment of the population may be viewed with distaste by another. Sometimes a disparity in views is due to differences in ethnic background, age, or sex. It is not such individual differences *per se* that cause the different reactions to touch, but rather, the meaning and evaluation given to the touch by one's culture or life situation. A study by Nguyen, Heslin, and Nguyen (1975), for example, found high agreement between males and females about whether a given type of touch—stroke, squeeze, pat, or brush (perhaps by accident)—to a given body area (hands, arms, back, genitals, etc.) indicated sexual desire on the part of the toucher ($r = +.94$). Yet for men the more a touch from their best friend of the opposite sex conveyed sexual desire, the more they considered it pleasant ($r = +.76$) and indicative of love ($r = +.60$). Women reacted to sexual touching in just the opposite manner ($r = -.74$ for pleasantness and $r = -.71$ for love). Subsequent research (Nguyen, Heslin, & Nguyen, 1976) was initiated to discover whether they had uncovered a bona fide difference between the sexes or whether it was due to the fact that the subjects in the 1975 study were unmarried freshmen and sophomores. They found that, compared to single men, married men were less enthusiastic about sexual touch ($r = +.34$ with pleasantness and $r = +.28$ with warmth and love), but married women showed a more positive attitude toward touch the more it meant sexual desire ($r = +.62$ with pleasantness and $r = +.73$ with love and warmth). It seems that some factor or factors affected by marriage (or by some similar long-term commitment) has a positive effect on women's attitude and a negative effect on men's attitude toward sexual touching.

Those associated with the human potential movement (encounter groups, etc.) have long maintained that touching leads to liking. This belief was put to the test in a setting divested of the encounter-group atmosphere. Using an "ESP experiment" as a subterfuge, it was found that female subjects who explored the face of a female confederate, and had their face explored by her, had a generally more positive attitude toward the confederate than subjects in a no-touch control condition (Boderman, Freed, & Kinnucan, 1972).

Thus we appear to have evidence that touching causes liking. However, in an attempt to replicate and extend this last study, Breed and Ricci (1973) proposed that the touch effect may have been due to greater confederate warmth in the touch condition. Therefore they manipulated warm or cold demeanor on the part of the confederate along with the touch and no-touch conditions. Subjects responded to the warmth and cold variations but not to the touch variations. Breed and Ricci concluded that there was a good possibility that the Boderman *et al.* effect was due to the confederate in the touch condition being warmer and more pleasant than in the no-touch condition. Consequently, touch *per se* may have had little or no effect on the subjects. While such an interpretation is certainly consistent with the Breed and Ricci (1973) results, it may still be the case that touching and communication of warmth and caring are inextricably intertwined. If that is so, then separating them is artificial and does not represent naturally occurring reality.

The problem with the Boderman experiments is that they were atypical experiences (to say the least) for the people in them, and susceptible to attempts by the subjects to: (1) act in a way that they considered expected of them as experimental subjects, or (2) try to behave and respond to questions so as to look healthy, bright, and well adjusted. A study by Fisher, Rytting, and Heslin (1976) is free of these contaminants. When clerks in a university library either touched or avoided touching the hand of a patron as they returned his or her identification card, this less than half-second touch caused the female patrons to like the clerk, feel better, and like the library better than those in the no-touch condition. This finding is a demonstration that casual touch by a stranger can be more positive than negative, and it has the power to influence a person's general sense of well-being.

It seems then that touching can lead to liking, but that the relationship between these two sets of variables is complex and susceptible to other influences such as warmth of the touch and the meaning assigned to it by the recipient. Let us now turn to the opposite side of the touching-liking relation: whether people are more likely to touch someone they like.

The evidence that liking leads to touching is sparse and comes from scattered sources. Most of it is correlational in nature. For example, Jourard (1966) found that college students touch and are touched on far more areas of their body by their best friend of the opposite sex than by their parents or best friend of the same sex. This would seem to indicate that these students touch and are touched by those with whom they have the strongest liking relationship. However, in interpreting Jourard's (1966) findings we cannot ignore the norm in American culture that one does not touch same-sex others or parents in more than a friendly way because of concern about incest and homosexuality. Also, since Heslin and Boss (1980) found a strong relationship between the intimacy of a relationship (which rated parent–child as high intimacy) and the intimacy of the touch used in greeting at an airport, it seems more likely that Jourard's dependent variable, the number of different areas of the body touched, influenced his findings.

One way of analyzing touch is in terms of the form and meaning of its use. Heslin (1974) has proposed five levels of relationships which classify the types and meanings of touch. First, the *professional/functional* level refers to the kinds of touch used by barbers, dentists, physicians, golf pros, and anyone who relates to the person as an object to which he is trying to do something. Such an interpretation of touch focuses on it as a means to some impersonal end. *Social/polite* touch involves recognizing the other person as a social being. For example, refusal to shake hands with another is considered to be a strong insult. Such a reaction implies that the refuser will not grant the other the status of personhood usually because of some strong negative feelings toward him or her. In general, a handshake serves to reduce animosity and status differences. *Friendship/warmth* is characterized by such touches as a squeeze on the arm or an arm around the shoulder. It indicates liking as distinguished from loving. *Love/intimacy* touch (kissing, holding hands, etc.) is considered appropriate if the relationship is deeper than mere friendship. *Sexual arousal* encompasses touch that conveys sexual arousal in the toucher and creates sexual arousal in the recipient.

Heslin (1974) proposed that there are two possible models of how the intimacy of the touching relates to liking. The first view is that there is a direct linear relationship between liking and touch intimacy. Thus increasingly intimate touching is a manifestation of increased liking and attraction. However, alternate views of liking or love might lead to the suggestion of a curvilinear relationship between intimacy of touch and liking. Specifically, as one moves to loving and sexual touch, and the role relations implied by each of them, the other person is in danger of being viewed less as a person and more as a "love object" or "sex object." Intimate touch under these circumstances may not reflect a true concern for the other person but merely serve more personal or selfish needs.

The research by Jourard (1966) on reported incidence of touch and by Heslin and Boss (1980) on the nature of touching at an airport focuses on how a relationship affects touching. A different way to consider the same question is to see what observers infer about a relationship from seeing interactions involving touch. In one such study, Kleinke, Meeker, and LaFong (1974) found that "engaged" couples who touched one another were rated more favorably (loving, etc.) than those who did not touch.

We can conclude this section on touching and liking by observing that there is indirect evidence of touching as a response to liking and of liking as a response to touching. However, the role of experimenter choice of touch conditions must be recognized. Experimenters have hesitated to investigate touch situations that would be likely to cause a negative reaction from their subjects. At this time we can say that there are some situations in which touching leads to positive response, and furthermore that some of these even include touch from strangers. But we must not forget that the right to touch another person is also a status-related prerogative. In chapter 3 we shall examine the issue in discussing proposals by Goffman and Henley concerning power and touching.

Other Nonverbal Behaviors

Facial Expressions.   Although research on facial expressions has a long history, facial expressions have seldom been studied as a determinant or manifestation of liking. This is strange because facial expressions are so visible and have been described as critical indicators of feelings (Ekman, Friesen, & Ellsworth, 1972; Tompkins, 1962). A great deal of research has been concerned with the dimensions of emotion expressed by the face (e.g., disgust, surprise, fear, etc.) and whether these facial expressions are learned or innate. However, very little has been done regarding facial expressions that may cause liking, despite such observations as Dale Carnegie's: "So if you want people to like you, *smile*."

There has been somewhat more evidence that people see facial expressions as *results* of variations in liking than as *causes* of liking. But one study gives some indirect indication of nonverbal behavior that might be both a cause and a result of liking. Rosenfeld (1966) asked undergraduates to behave in a way with other undergraduates so as to gain or avoid their approval. He found that the approval seekers were significantly higher than approval avoiders in percentage of smiles. We are not sure whether this indicates that people assume that smiling will make them likable (cause liking), or that someone from whom they would want approval should be someone they would like and that such liking would be manifested by smiling.

At the same time it is also clear that smiling does not always reflect a positive feeling state. For example, there is some evidence, at least for women, that smiling may often be a manifestation of discomfort and deference (Beeman, 1975). Further, people may smile more when they are attempting to deceive others (Mehrabian, 1971). Obviously, we can use facial expressions to cover feelings we do not wish revealed.

Gestures, Body Orientation, and Lean. Mehrabian (1969b) has proposed that forward lean and direct body orientation are components of his "immediacy" factor—an index of attraction and intimacy. In contrast, Rosenfeld (1965) found no differences in the angle of orientation a subject used in trying to seek approval versus avoid approval from another person. Forward lean was also used by Reece and Whitman (1962), in combination with a smile, keeping hands still, and eye contact to convey a warm experimenter attitude. Although they found that the "warm" combination of nonverbal behaviors was reinforcing to others, they did not examine which of the behaviors was more reinforcing than the others. However, a recent study by Trout and Rosenfeld (1980) varied forward lean independently in a videotape of a "therapist" and "client." Forward lean had a significant effect on ratings of rapport.

Although it appears that forward lean and a direct body orien-

tation are related to liking, there are exceptions to such a generali-
zation. For example, Mehrabian (1969a) found that men use more
direct orientation toward *disliked* males than do females. Mehrabian
interpreted this difference in terms of greater potential threat to men
from other disliked men, with corresponding increased tension and
vigilance. An equally plausible explanation of the difference could be
due to the fact that dominant and intimate nonverbal behaviors—for
example, gazing, close personal space, and touching—convey both
liking and superior status, depending on the situation. With cross-
sex interaction, men may interpret these behaviors from women as
indicating attraction rather than dominance, presumably because
dominance from women is threatening to men (Henley, 1977). If direct
body orientation can be interpreted as a sign of either dominance or
attraction, men will feel free to face a disliked male directly because
an attraction interpretation is not likely to be made; however, women
will avoid facing a disliked male directly because of the likelihood
that it would be interpreted by the male recipient as a manifestation
of attraction.

Paralanguage.   Although a fair amount of research has been
directed toward understanding paralanguage (vocal inflections, speech
errors, speech rate, etc.) it shares with facial expression the position
of being relatively underresearched in the area of interpersonal liking.
Paralanguage is an amazingly subtle and powerful tool for communication. It may be second only to facial expression in being able to
convey liking for another (Mehrabian & Ferris, 1967; Mehrabian &
Wiener, 1967). Mehrabian (1972) proposed that the components contributing to liking were as follows: Total liking = 7% verbal liking,
+ 38% vocal liking, + 55% facial liking. Although this proposed
weighting is interesting, one would be ill advised to try to generalize
these results to real conversations without further research. Bugental,
Kaswan, and Love (1970) found that children, compared to adults,
attend more to the *verbal* than to the facial expression that goes with
it (e.g., in the case of criticism with a smile). In other words, they
cannot understand sarcasm or "take a joke" that is made at their
expense. However, in support of Mehrabian's suggestion, the facial
channel was found to receive greater weight in the resolution of conflicting messages than either the verbal or vocal channels.

There are other ways in which paralanguage relates to liking. For
example, a person with an accent will be liked less than a person

without an accent (e.g., Ryan & Carranza, 1975). In addition, a person's rate of speech can influence how much he or she is liked. Kleinke, Staneski, and Berger (1975), for example, found that subjects preferred interviewers who had high rates of talking to those with low rates of talking. Weitz (1972) found that the warmth of a white person's tone of voice as he read instructions to a black person related positively to the friendliness of behavior in the form of the white person volunteering for extra hours of work with that black, whereas a paper-and-pencil measure of liking for the black person was *negatively* related to the amount of time the white person volunteered to work. We have here a good illustration of paralanguage as an index of latent conflict between negative feelings and the wish to appear in a socially desirable light. The use of paralanguage as a more valid indicator of feelings than verbal report is one of the most fascinating areas of nonverbal behavior.

The communication of liking through nonverbal paralanguage is complicated by the fact that love turns out to be one of the hardest feelings to communicate with voice alone, whereas anger has been found to be the easiest—judges have the greatest difficulty identifying the emotion when someone is trying to convey love (Davitz & Davitz, 1959).

Mixed Nonverbal Behavior. Since similarity in attitude has been found to lead to attraction, one might expect similarity in nonverbal behavior to lead to liking. Dabbs (1969) found that when a confederate mimicked one of a pair of subjects (leaning forward, erect, crossing arms or legs, touching shoes, fidgeting, etc.), those who were mimicked liked the confederate more and gave him higher ratings on "well informed," "sound ideas," and "good presentation of ideas" than nonmimicked subjects. Thus, adopting the posture, facial expression, and gestures of others enhances the impression they have of the mimicker. Similarly, Bates (1976) found college students reacting much more positively toward a seventh-grade confederate who imitated the moves they were teaching in a basketball skill situation than toward a confederate who did not. The college students manifested the liking by verbal and nonverbal means (e.g., closer distance, more gazing, and shift in positivity of tone). There is some difficulty in interpreting their results, however, because the mimicking was also instrumental to task accomplishment for the college students. The study by Trout and Rosenfeld (1980) mentioned above in connection with the effect of forward lean does not have the ambiguity presented by the Bates (1976) study. They manipulated whether their "therapist" showed congruence with the "client" in placement of arms and legs. Therapists who were congruent with their client were rated as having more rapport with their clients than those who did not arrange their arms and legs in the same way as their client.

Conclusions

From the viewpoint of an observer, touching, standing close, gazing, smiling, and leaning forward are seen as indications of attraction or of a close social relationship between the people observed. Even from the viewpoint of the actor, these nonverbal behaviors probably are seen as indicating attraction in most situations, though the actor may not always be aware of the link between his or her behavior and attraction. It is from the viewpoint of the recipient that different meanings can often develop, leading to very distinct and contrasting reactions.

Although these nonverbal behaviors are attraction indicators, there is some question about whether they are attraction evokers. The delicate balance between intimacy and invasion of privacy is difficult to maintain in interpersonal relations, and some of these nonverbal behaviors can be particularly intrusive and offensive when they are not desired by the recipient. It is expected that some of the most fruitful work regarding attraction and nonverbal behavior will deal with this bipolarity of intimacy and privacy invasion.

CHAPTER 3

The Role of Nonverbal Cues in Social Influence

Nonverbal behavior is relevant to social influence for some of the same reasons that it is relevant to interpersonal attraction; furthermore, attraction is one of the major facilitators of influence.

In time of emotional upheaval, words—especially written words—can become less important than usual, and people who are skilled in manipulating the nonverbal and symbolic become important. In 1936, Schuman wrote that Adolph Hitler

> had an intuitive feeling for what was effective in propaganda. But he wrote badly and was never at home in the world of written words. . . . For him the spoken word was always to be preferred to writing. He was a spellbinder, not a journalist. (p. 82)

He was even better in communicating through use of the symbolic and visual:

> He invented the *Hakenkreuz* flag and much of the elaborate military insignia of the S.A. and S.S. . . . He was the symbol artist *par excellence*. At the time of the Nürnberg convention of 1927 he spent three days in meditation and then emerged with the striking *Partei-Tag Plakate*. He was actor and stage director, as well as scene painter, costumer, and property man. The pageantry of the great parades and mass meetings was his. The regimented, inspired storm troopers parading with flags and standards through flagged streets and down the aisles of bannered halls to the crash of martial music were his. The impressive *Fahnenweihe* ceremony was his. In its performance he walked down the ranked rows of S.A. standards and flags and touched each one solemnly and mysteriously with the sacred *Blutfahne* of 1923, the tattered banner stained with the blood of the martyrs who fell before the *Felderrnhalle*. (p. 81)

Thus in the end the persuasiveness of the Nazis was less in what they wrote than in what they said, and less in what they said than in what they did and how they did it. Their impact was enhanced by their clever use of the nonverbal side of behavior in addition to the verbal. This was illustrated in their growing demonstration of power and solidarity as wave after wave of storm troopers marched through the streets, as *Sieg Heil* was chanted over and over, washing over opposition and reaffirming the faith of the devoted (Bosmajian, 1971).

This description of Hitler's impact represents an extreme but telling example of the way in which patterns of nonverbal behavior can sway the masses. Most of our discussion will not be focusing on such occurrences of mass persuasion or influence, but the magnitude of the effects, even on only one or two people in social interaction, is often a similarly substantial one.

The role of the nonverbal dimension in persuasion has probably been underestimated simply because persuasion has been studied in an artificial laboratory or classroom setting by academics, who, as a group, are highly verbal people. But in reality most decisions are not made in response to a persuasive communication. Most decisions are made in response to such things as a desire to be like someone else, fear of rejection by one's associates, fear of financial loss, or a reluctance to expend any more than the very minimum in time and energy. We often try to gauge the level of honesty, desperation, and sophistication of a communicator. Thus, a communicator's nonverbal behavior has the potential of helping the listener evaluate both the communicator and the communication.

DECEPTION

There is a general belief that one should trust the nonverbal message when it does not seem to agree with what is being said. To varying degrees people seem to agree with Freud (1905/1959): "He that has eyes to see and ears to hear may convince himself that no mortal can keep a secret. If his lips are silent, he chatters with his finger tips; betrayal oozes out of him at every pore." It is easier to lie and say no than to keep from blushing or to keep one's hands from shaking.

The nonverbal behaviors that people display while they are lying may reflect, among other states, one or more of the following: (1) their true feelings, (2) poorly executed attempts at deception, (3) appropriate or inappropriate anxiety or doubt, or (4) feelings completely unrelated to the present situation. The person's true feelings (e.g., anger, depression, love, superiority) may be manifested in vocal characteristics, posture, gaze, or other behaviors. Poorly executed attempts at deception are sometimes manifested by exaggerated responses and inappropriate elements in a response, such as a person smiling too much when he really feels superior to the other person. Anxiety about being caught is more likely to be present where there is some negative sanction associated with either the substance of the lie or lying itself. Finally, we should also stress that habitual differences in many behaviors, perhaps related to personality or other individual difference variables, may account for an isolated pattern of behavior. In this last case we would be wrong to infer that such behavior reflects anything reliable about deception.

An early study in this area was reported by Ekman and Friesen (1969a). They had judges view silent films of people being interviewed. Although the judges did not know it, the people in the film were patients who were known to be hiding their true feelings about problems they had. Some of the judges saw only the faces of the patients, others saw only the neck down, and others saw the whole person. Since Ekman and Friesen reported on only three examples of deception, two of which were with the same patient, any generalizations made from their findings must be made with caution. However, the findings on these two patients indicated that observers who saw only the face were deceived more often than those who saw the body. One patient who was denying feelings of anxiety and confusion was rated by those who saw her face as cooperative, cheerful, pleasant, and so forth, while those who saw only her body rated her as tense, nervous, defensive, and cautious. Clearly two quite distinct channels of information were being transmitted by this patient, and the lower body information seemed to be closer to the feelings she was trying to deny to herself and hide from others.

Ekman and Friesen proposed that, compared to the hands and feet, the face has greater sending capacity in terms of being faster, more varied, subtle, and more visible to a recipient. In addition, the face generates more feedback from the recipient and gives better internal feedback to the sender. Because of these differences, people are more likely to be aware of their facial impressions and of the attention being given to them by the other person. Furthermore, the senders should be able to recall what their facial expressions are when they really feel the emotion they are now trying to simulate. In general, neither the communicator nor the observer are aware of the trunk and legs, and because of this communicators are either unmotivated or unable to use these parts of the body in deception. The hands are apparently somewhere between the face and feet in saliency for deceptive communications.

Ekman and Friesen also make a distinction between movements of the feet or legs and posture, even though both kinds of nonverbal behavior are less reactive and subtle than paralanguage and facial expression. It is their contention that posture is much more socially dictated and a function of one's role and therefore fairly easy to simulate when one wishes to deceive another. The basic tenet of Ekman and Friesen's position is that the more a nonverbal behavior is usually ignored, the better a cue to deception it is. The strength of that tenet is open to testing by research. Indeed, a recent study (Ekman, Friesen, O'Sullivan, & Scherer, 1980) seems to indicate that the tenet is not as strong or solid as Ekman and Friesen originally assumed it to be.

One of the common assumptions regarding deception is that honest people are more likely to "look you in the eye," and a person who is deceiving you is more likely to avoid your eyes. Explanation for this expectation usually includes the fact that the person who is deceiving is feeling uneasy about deceiving, anxious about possible discovery and the visibility of anxiety, and unsure about the appropriate behaviors to display in trying to appear natural and honest. Such feelings might be expected to lead to a decrease in gazing toward the listener. If the recipient, in turn, is scrutinizing the deceiver closely, such scrutiny could confound the deceiver even more, increase anxiety, and cause greater behavioral discomfort. Finally, if one is concentrating hard on talking or lying, it is easier to do it if one blocks out distractions by looking less at the listener. Are these intuitive guesses correct? We will discuss some of the research on these issues and try to answer that question.

A study by Exline, Thibaut, Hickey, and Gumpert (1970) examined the hypothesis that people avoid the eyes of another person when they are deceiving. In that study subjects were induced to cheat on an experimental task by their partner, who was really a confederate of the experimenter. Then the experimenter came back into the room, completed the task, and interviewed the subject. During the interview the experimenter gradually "became suspicious." He accused the subject of cheating. Subject's eye behavior was recorded by film and evaluated throughout the course of the interview, which included a baseline period and the eventual accusation of cheating. Figure 3 shows the number of seconds per minute the subject looked at the experimenter. People who had cheated looked at the experimenter less than they had before cheating. However, when high-Machiavellian subjects (high scorers on a scale that measures tendency to use other people for one's own purposes) who had cheated were confronted, they *increased* the amount of time they looked at the in-

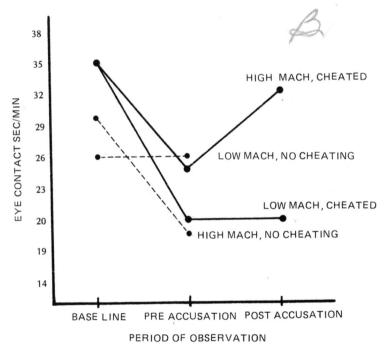

Figure 3. Period of observation: eye contact as a function of Machiavellianism and cheating (Exline *et al.* 1970).

terviewer, yielding a significant ($p < .05$) difference between them and the low-Machiavellian subjects after accusation. Although the effect was not strong and bears replication (e.g., see Knapp, Hart, & Dennis, 1974 below) it does suggest that different kinds of people respond differently to a deception situation.

In another study, nonverbal correlates of deception were noted when subjects argued against positions they either supported or opposed (Mehrabian, 1971). When subjects were deceiving the audience about their true beliefs, they talked less, more slowly, and with more errors, they moved their body less, they smiled more, they leaned or turned away from the audience more, and they looked at the audience less. In summary, this overall behavioral pattern seemed to indicate the presence of conflict, less efficient communication, and reduced interpersonal immediacy.

A study by Knapp, Hart, and Dennis (1974) had military veterans respond to a trained interviewer by arguing for increased veterans' benefits for education in one session and against increasing the benefits at a second session. When videotapes of the subjects were analyzed it was found that when the veterans were deceiving (compared to when they were telling the truth), they manifested: (1) significantly more time in nonverbal adaptor behavior ("fidgeting" with clothing, pencils, face, etc.), (2) less time gazing at the interviewer, and (3) fewer words. It is also interesting to note some verbal differences. Deceivers used fewer different words, fewer factual statements, and fewer group references (we, our, etc.). They used more leveling terms (all, nobody, etc.), more references to "others" (they, them, etc.), more disparaging remarks ("Those veterans are already using their benefits to rip off the government."), and they required more probing questions from the interviewer to keep things moving. We can see from this study that deceivers differed from nondeceivers in showing behaviors that reflect uncertainty, vagueness, nervousness, and reticence. However, a number of expected differences were not found. For example, deceivers did not make more speech errors or show more leg movements. They also did not pause more than nondeceivers. Yet, out of 32 variables studied, 26 were in the predicted direction. The authors also investigated the role of Machiavellianism on behavior in a deception situation and did not find Machiavellian subjects to be better than non-Machiavellian subjects in controlling their nonverbal behavior.

This latter finding is in conflict with the Exline, Thibaut, Hickey, and Gumpert (1970) finding that Machiavellian subjects increased gaze when attempting to cover their cheating. While such inconsistencies have to be expected in research on any complicated issue, there is some convergence over the results from different studies. First, deception usually leads to some behaviorally manifested discomfort. Changed behavioral patterns often occur in attempted deception either because of the stress or anxiety or in an attempt to cover those reactions. Finally, personality differences may moderate how well someone manages an incident of deception.

INTERPERSONAL INFLUENCE AND NONVERBAL BEHAVIOR

Body Posture and Gestures

Scheflen (1965; Scheflen & Scheflen, 1972) describes the matching of nonverbal behaviors as one aspect of indicating positive attitude toward another and shared orientation. Dabbs (1969) investigated the effect of mimicking another's posture and gestures in two separate studies. In the first study he used a trained actor who talked with a pair of male undergraduates and mimicked (not in the derisive sense) the posture and some of the gestures of one of them during their conversation. Dabbs found that the mimicked subject liked the confederate more than did the other subject. The mimicked subject felt that the confederate was better informed, had sounder ideas, and presented his ideas better than did the nonmimicked subject. In the second study, one subject was instructed to "antimimic" the behavior of the other subject, that is, choose behaviors and a bodily orientation that were opposite to those used by the other subject. It was found that if the antimimicking person was similar to him, the person who had been antimimicked indicated low liking for the confederate. Apparently, getting dissimilar behavior when one might expect similar behavior (as from a similar other) is discomforting. More recently, mimicking has been investigated as a manifestation of "congruence" between a therapist and client (Trout & Rosenfeld, 1980). When judges viewed videotapes of the middle and lower bodies of a "therapist" and "client," they attributed greater rapport to the situations in which the limbs of the therapist matched those of the client and when the therapist and client leaned forward. Similarly, many of us have noted that when we talk on the telephone with people we have not seen in a while, such as parents who are living far away, we fall into a pattern of speaking and accent such that a spouse or friend who knows us well can guess to whom we are speaking. We have different styles with different friends and acquaintances—jocular, serious, parental, seductive, very polite, or authoritative. Mimicking seems to be a nonverbal technique that people use to enhance their apparent similarity to others.

Are there any particular body movements or postures that seem to be associated with persuasiveness, separate from the question of whether or not they mimic the other person? A study to investigate "open" and "closed" body orientations was conducted by McGinley, LeFevre, and McGinley (1975). They found that communicators who were pictured in open body positions (limbs outward) were evaluated more positively than those in a closed body position, and they obtained greater opinion change than communicators depicted in closed or neutral positions. Earlier, Mehrabian and Williams (1969) had attempted to discover nonverbal concomitants of perceived and intended persuasiveness. They conducted three experiments which involved attempts of students to inform or persuade their peers. In the first study three groups of subjects were formed. One was told to argue with a high degree of persuasive intent, the second was instructed to use a moderate degree of persuasiveness, and the third was instructed to be neutral and not persuasive. Each subject took 10 minutes to prepare and then deliver a presentation to a confederate while being recorded by a hidden videotape recorder. The experimenters found that increased persuasiveness was related to a more upright posture, increased head nods, and more frequent hand gestures. In general it appears that subjects instructed to be more persuasive showed more energy and were more involved in the interaction. In the second study Mehrabian and Williams manipulated intended persuasiveness by giving instructions to "be persuasive" or "be informative." Furthermore, audience receptivity was varied by

having the confederate appear to be either "receptive" or "nonrecep-
tive" to the message. The subject presented a communication to the
confederate while being observed through a one-way mirror. Anal-
yses were made of nonverbal behaviors as a function of degree of
intended persuasiveness, sex of the subject, and nonverbal receptivity
of the listener.

There were no main effects for intent to persuade on gestures,
movements, or body postures. However, the amount that speakers
swiveled in their chairs was a joint function of their sex and the degree
of the speaker's earnestness in trying to persuade the recipient. Women
swiveled less when they were trying to change the recipient's view.
That is, when they were working at being persuasive, women inhibited extraneous movements. The receptivity of the listener and the
persuasive-informative manipulation affected how often (and how
long) speakers touched themselves: if the listeners were receptive to
subjects who were trying hard to persuade, they touched themselves
as they talked; if the listeners were not receptive to them, they touched
themselves less.

In the third experiment, Mehrabian and Williams shifted from
varying the persuasiveness of the speakers and noting their nonverbal
behavior to varying the nonverbal behavior of the speaker (distance,
eye contact, shoulder orientation, and postural relaxation) and rating
his or her persuasiveness. Subjects rated on a 7-point scale of convincingness 256 30-second segments of videotape with the audio
turned off. A number of variables affected perceived convincingness
of the speaker, but we shall concentrate on those that deal with body
orientation and gestures as depicted in Table 2. With male communicators they found an indirect shoulder orientation (30°) to be more
persuasive than a frontal orientation. They also found a general tendency in both sexes for very relaxed body positions to result in low-
convincingness ratings. However, female communicators who were
more tense were more convincing, while male communicators who
were slightly relaxed were most convincing.

Mehrabian and Williams found support for the general hypothesis that cues to liking would be associated with perceived persuasiveness. Yet, cues to liking a recipient were also associated with
decreased dominance. It would seem, then, that prestige, expertise, and
status—which have been considered to be aspects of source credibil-

Table 2. Significant Determinants of Perceived Persuasiveness.[a]

Variable	F		Mean perceived persuasiveness	
			Direct	Indirect
Shoulder orientation	29		1.81	1.90
Shoulder orientation by communicator sex	73	Male	1.78	1.97
		Female	1.80	1.82
		Slightly tense	Slightly relaxed	Moderately relaxed	Very relaxed
Postural relaxation	208	2.10	2.46	1.65	1.20
Postural relaxation by communicator sex	Male 138	1.95	2.69	1.64	1.24
	Female	2.25	2.23	1.67	1.17

[a] Based on Mehrabian & Williams (1969).

ity—may work against actual persuasiveness if they are manifested nonverbally in a manner that decreases liking for that person. The nonverbal behaviors that are associated with source dominance or status (e.g., fewer head nods, less smiling) are also associated with not liking the recipient.

Paralanguage

One of the earliest studies of vocal style was conducted by Woolbert (1920). He found that large variations in pitch, volume, speed, and quality of voice resulted in better retention of the material than no variation. Except for an occasional finding in support of Woolbert (e.g., Glasgow, 1952), the greatest reaction to unvarying speech has been found to be distaste rather than inability to remember what was said. Research on variety in paralinguistic characteristics of speech have usually failed to find variation in vocal quality affecting either comprehension (e.g., Diehl, White, & Satz, 1961) or recall (Utzinger, 1952). As with life, variety may be the spice, but the information is the basic sustenance, and it usually gets through whether it is made more palatable or not.

If a varying voice has only a weak effect, is there any characteristic of the sound of a speaker that influences the communication process? One comparison of different qualities found no effect of harshness or hoarseness but did find that breathy or nasal speech reduced comprehension (Diehl & McDonald, 1956).

A study by Addington (1971) typifies one approach to research on paralanguage and speaker credibility. He had the same message taped by 10 female speakers. Before recording each speech, each speaker practiced delivering it according to a given paralinguistic dimension. The 15 dimensions actually studied can be grouped into four different categories: (1) speaking rate, (2) pitch variety, (3) voice quality, and (4) articulation. A total of 180 students rated 10 speeches apiece on a number of semantic-differential scales that measured: (1) competence (experienced–inexperienced, expert–ignorant, etc.); (2) dynamism (energetic–tired, bold–timid, etc.); and (3) trustworthiness (kind–cruel, honest–dishonest, etc.). The normal and slow presentations received the highest overall credibility, followed closely by the varied pitch and the fast speeches. The lowest credibility ratings were given to the speaker with poor articulation and throaty presentation. Almost as low in credibility were the nasal, monotone, tense, "denasal", throaty, and breathy speakers.

How is source credibility affected by nonfluencies (e.g., stammer, sentence change, word repetition, omissions, and "ah" or similar sound)? Early findings indicated that the various kinds of nonfluencies do not all have the same effect on impressions of the speaker. For example, saying "ah" was far less damaging than stammering or repeating words (Miller & Hewgill, 1964). However, in general, as interruptions increased, ratings of competency of the speaker decreased. But even if speakers trip over their words, all is not lost. Although people may see the speaker as less competent, they may still be influenced by the message (Sereno & Hawkins, 1967). That finding is consonant with something that Addington (1971) had discovered in his study—that only competence, not trustworthiness, was affected by paralinguistic cues.

It is likely that the manner of presentation may enhance some aspects of credibility such as enthusiasm and commitment, while at the same time detracting from other aspects such as objectivity and trustworthiness. A study by Pearce and Conklin (1971) is relevant to such a problem. Judges listened to an electronically muffled voice of a speaker whose delivery was either calm or emotional. The emotional voice had more variation in rate and pitch and had a higher tone and volume than the calm voice. The judges saw the emotional speaker as more assertive, self-assured, tough-minded, and task-oriented. However, the judges saw the calm, objective speaker as more trustworthy, likable, attractive, honest, and people-oriented, as well as better educated, richer, and taller. Thus each style was credible in its own way.

The Pearce and Conklin study had varied the emotionality of a speech and assessed the paralinguistic differences between the calm and emotional delivery. In a related investigation Scherer, London, and Wolf (1973) examined the effect of a confident versus doubtful speaking style. Computer analysis of the voice pattern indicated that speakers talked faster and louder and had shorter pauses when they were expressing confidence rather than doubt. Judges rated the speaker whose voice was confident as being more enthusiastic, forceful, and dominant. In a more recent study (Apple, Streeter, & Krauss, 1979), greater control over the vocal characteristics of the speaker was obtained than in the earlier studies. This greater control was made possible by digitizing the spoken material and analyzing it into loudness and pitch components over time. When pitch was varied independently of speech and volume, the researchers found deviation from normal pitch and speed resulted in negative evaluations of their (male) speakers, with high-pitched and slow-talking speakers being rated most negatively.

The ability to so use one's voice so that the meaning is accurately perceived is only half of the communication problem. The person listening to that voice may be skilled or unskilled in decoding paralinguistic cues. J.A. Hall (1980) found that sending ability by itself was not related to social influence, but the combination of good senders plus good decoders gave the most positive influence (i.e., in the direction of the influence attempt).

In general, it appears that a variety of paralinguistic cues can have substantial effects on the impression a speaker gives; for example, slower speech, stuttering, nasality, and speech errors usually lead to more negative impressions of the speaker. However, response to such speech patterns are not clearly related to the response to speech content *per se*. Apparently, some cues related to impressions of increased competence may simultaneously decrease a speaker's trustworthiness, for example, an emotional voice as in the Pearce and

Conklin (1971) study. Thus contrasting speech patterns may yield very different speaker impressions but produce similar effects on reactions to the content of the speaker's message.

Gazing Behavior

Gazing apparently has three social functions. The first is monitoring the other person to facilitate the flow of conversation, for example, to know when he or she wants to speak. The second function is to inform the gazer about the affective state of the other person, for example, whether the listener has taken offense at what was just said. The third (and most mystical) function of gazing is to indicate the gazer's feelings to the other person. The belief that an honest person looks you in the eye reflects such a notion.

Let us first look at the effect which variable amounts of gazing have on impression formation. There are two kinds of responses to a communicator which interest us here. One deals with the speaker's attractiveness to the audience and the other focuses on the speaker's credibility. It appears that we know more about the effect of gazing on liking than on any other aspect of the influence process. Further, it is obvious that someone whom we like has an increased degree of influence on us. However, what are the more direct effects of gazing on influencing others? The Mehrabian and Williams (1969) study discussed earlier is particularly relevant. In that study, subjects who had been instructed to use a neutral manner in their presentation looked at the recipient only 40% of the time, those instructed to be moderately persuasive looked 44% of the time, while those instructed to be highly persuasive looked 51% of the time. This effect of intended persuasiveness on eye contact was replicated in a second study reported in the same article. People in the "information only" presentation looked only 36% of the time, and those in the "persuasiveness" presentation looked 47% of the time. In their third experiment, Mehrabian and Williams reversed the direction of inquiry by instructing models on how to manage their body movement and gazing during videotaped presentation. The effects of the various manipulated conditions were determined on rating of perceived persuasiveness. Although the effects were statistically significant, in practical terms they were not very large. Nevertheless, the sex of subject by gaze-level interaction showed that women were seen as more persuasive when they employed high gaze, while men were seen as more persuasive when they employed a moderate level of gaze. A second three-way interaction involves sex of subject, gaze level, and distance (see Figure 4). Although speakers were perceived as more persuasive at the closer distance, that effect was qualified by amount of gaze and sex of speaker. Specifically, males were seen as consistently more persuasive than females at the closer distance under moderate- and high-gaze conditions, but as less persuasive than females in the distant, high-gaze condition.

The Mehrabian and Williams study examined intended and perceived persuasiveness as a function of nonverbal behavior. In a related investigation of credibility, Beebe (1974) hypothesized a direct relationship between manipulated gaze level and speaker credibility. Beebe and his subjects rate the speakers on three factor-analytically

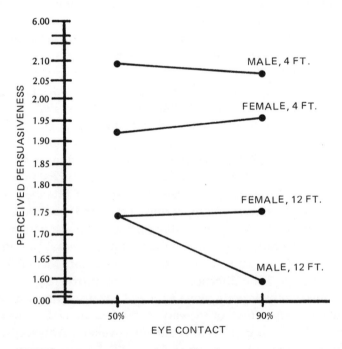

Figure 4. The effect of percentage of gazing time, communicator sex, and distance on perceived pursuasiveness. Based on Mehrabian & Williams (1969).

derived speaker credibility scales: qualification, dynamism, and honesty. He found ratings on speaker qualification to be significantly affected by the amount of gaze at the audience. Both high- and moderate-eye-contact speakers were significantly more credible than the no-eye-contact speaker. The dynamism factor was not significantly affected by eye contact, but the honesty factor was. In general, this study supported the folk belief that low eye contact by a speaker means decreased credibility. The association of credibility with gazing has also been reported elsewhere (Exline, 1972).

We have looked at the role of gazing on a communicator's credibility and on an audience's stated willingness to believe his or her statements. But has gaze been shown to have any effect on whether someone actually believes or conforms to another's wishes? Again, the data are indirect and suggestive. One study examined the effect of gaze in influencing cooperative behavior in the prisoner's dilemma game (a bargaining situation that poses a dilemma to a participant: the subject must decide whether to trust that the other person will not take advantage of the subject's trusting gesture). Persons who experienced the confederate's gaze had a higher heart rate than those who were not the objects of gaze. Although arousal level was increased by gaze, those subjects were not any more cooperative than subjects in the no-gaze condition, regardless of whether the confederate acted cooperatively or competitively as the game progressed (Kleinke & Pohlen, 1971). Thus gazing physiologically affected the other person, but it did not alter the overall level of cooperation. More recently Kleinke (1980) has found gaze to increase the level of compliance with a request to return money left in a pay telephone by the previous user.

If gazing does influence the reactions of others toward the gazer, how does it happen? What mediates the initiation of gaze in affecting a particular response? Duval and Wicklund (1972; Wicklund, 1975) have proposed a way of considering how people respond to a number of social events, such as being the targets of a stare. They have termed the person's reaction *objective self-awareness*, a feeling that is akin to self-consciousness. One of the hypothesized results of heightened objective self-awareness is an attempt to live up to one's idealized self-image. An example of such a self-awareness response to gaze can be found in a study by Kleck, Vaughan, Cartwright-Smith, Vaughan,

Colby, and Lanzetta (1976). In that study, they found that observed subjects did not display the pain they were feeling as much as those who were not observed. Apparently when the subjects realized they were being watched, they tried to enact a more desirable presentation, that is, not show pain. We shall most probably see further exploration of the role of objective self-awareness in responding to gazing. The research examined in this analysis of gazing indicates that both what looking implies about the looker and its effects on the target person make gazing a meaningful topic for research and on social influence. The research also makes it fairly clear that the relation between influence and gazing is dependent on a variety of factors that give meaning to the gazing.

Distance

During police interrogations, spatial invasion is common. Texts on police methods recommends that the suspect not be placed behind a desk or even a desk chair. An obstruction of any sort gives the subject a feeling of relief and confidence not otherwise attainable. Although the officer may start the interrogation 2 or 3 feet away from the suspect, he is instructed to move his chair in close so that ultimately one of the suspect's knees is just about in between the interrogator's two knees. It is the clear implication that such close proximity makes the suspect more likely to yield to the officer's pressure to confess. Further, it is assumed that the close proximity will make guilty persons squirm as they sense they will not be able to hide the behavioral manifestations of guilt from the intense (and close) examination of the police officer.

Police officers have reported that they place a great deal of importance on nonverbal behavior in trying to understand and predict another person's behavior. Another person's posture, facial expression, eye behavior, and vocal characteristics have been reported to be important cues in forming an impression of a potential suspect (Rozelle & Baxter, 1975). While a variety of behaviors indicating stress or anxiety might serve to predict guilt, some of these reactions might simply be a result of discomfort from the overly close proximity of another person. Spatial invasion has been found to cause innocent people to manifest nonverbal behaviors that indicate both uneasiness and apparent guilt (Baxter & Rozelle, 1975). These nonverbal responses to spatial invasion include reactions such as: eyebrow movement plus gaze aversion, arms crossed across crotch, increased small movements of the head plus head rotation, increased trunk rotation, and decreased foot movement.

Close approaches can make another person uncomfortable, but can they increase one's influence over that person? Milgram (1965) found that compliance to an apparently unethical act (shocking another "subject") increased the closer the experimenter was to the subject. Whether this effect was due to the closer persuader being able to exert better surveillance over the recipient or to some other factor is uncertain. However, such increased influence at closer distances is consistent with results of the Mehrabian and Williams study discussed earlier.

What about a situation in which a person is simply asking another for a favor? Is physical proximity or distance likely to increase the chances of receiving help? Some information on this question is given from a study (Baron & Bell, 1976) in which men and women asked students if they would be willing to participate in a survey of student attitudes and opinions. The person could refuse to volunteer or volunteer for from ½ to 2½ hours. The requesters either stood at a distance of 3 to 4 feet (far condition) or 1 to 1½ feet (near condition). In the near condition, they placed their arms on the subject's table and leaned toward him or her while making the request. Respondents volunteered for more hours when the requester stood at a closer distance than when he or she approached them only at the far condition. Yet the subjects in the near condition described themselves as more calm and more comfortable than did those in the far condition. At the same time the near condition was seen as too close by those subjects.

Baron and Bell propose two possible explanations for the greater effectiveness of close approach compared to a more normal distance. First, the recipient might interpret that the requester felt friendlier toward him or her in the near condition than in the far condition and therefore reciprocate the liking in some way by volunteering more time. A second explanation they proposed was that because invasion of another's space is a violation that people take pains to avoid (cf. Efran & Cheyne, 1974; Fisher & Byrne, 1975), then the subject may interpret that invasion as evidence that the requester is in dire need of help. Either of these explanations is compatible with the finding of greater volunteering to the close requester.

To help decide which of these explanations was correct (or whether neither or both were correct), a second study was conducted that was very similar to the first. To check on the explanation that the close requester appeared more friendly than the one at the normal distance, the subjects were asked to rate the requester after she left (they used only female requesters in the second study because sex of requester had not had an effect in the first study). The requester who stood close was *not* seen as more or less friendly than the one who stood at the normal distance. To check on the second possible explanation, subjects were asked to rate the requester on her apparent need of assistance. The requester who stood close to make her request was rated as more in need of help than those who stood at 3 or 4 feet. Thus the desperation explanation seems the most likely.

A counterintuitive finding obtained in this research was that subjects in the close condition felt calmer and more comfortable than those in the far condition. As indicated in chapter 2, the usual response to spatial invasion includes both discomfort and emotional arousal. Baron and Bell proposed that the calm and comfort felt by the subjects in the near condition may have been the result of self-reinforcement resulting from the feeling of pride in having helped someone else. Consistent with this explanation were the positive correlations between length of time volunteered and calm feelings ($r = +.36$) and length of time volunteered and comfort feelings ($r = +.23$). There are, of course, alternate explanations for the positive feelings generated in the close condition. One would focus on the feelings of calmness and comfort resulting from being assured that the request was really needed and the volunteering of time was appropriate. The fact of the close approach, given the norm against it, may provide evidence for assuring subjects that the request was in fact a worthy one. Thus, such an explanation would focus on the removal of doubt about volunteering time, rather than the self-reinforcement produced by actually volunteering the time. Independent of the specific processes operating here, we might conclude that close approaches seem to increase the probability of successfully enlisting help.

Perhaps the clearest test of the effect of distance on persuasion found results that were at variance with those obtained by Baron and Bell (1976), Mehrabian and Williams (1969), and Milgram (1965). In this study (Albert & Dabbs, 1970) subjects were either 1 to 2, 4 to 5, or 14 to 15 feet from a speaker. Both were seated at a table, and the speaker used either a friendly or hostile manner in talking to the subject. The experimenters contrasted three possible models of reactions to interactions at unusual distances. First, there is the invasion of privacy model, which emphasizes the negative aspect of close proximity (Garfinkel, 1964; Sommer, 1966). Second, there is the position that emphasizes that proximity is associated with liking (Little, 1965; Mehrabian, 1968b; Rosenfeld, 1965). And third, there is the notion emphasized by Hall (1966) that there are zones of appropriate distance for a given kind of interaction, and when the distance is inappropriate for the interaction in either direction, the participants will feel uneasy or distracted.

The results showed some support for the view that there are zones of appropriate distance. Specifically, at the intermediate distance more attention was paid to the content of the speech, while at the near or far distances more attention was paid to the physical appearance of the speaker. However, attitude change itself increased with increased distance, a finding inconsistent with the Baron and Bell (1976) results. Thus there was no support for the moderate distance being most appropriate and therefore influencing subjects most.

As it sometimes happens in research, the end product of attitude change was obtained without correlated changes in factors apparently related to the attitude change. Communicators were not seen as more bold or aggressive when they sat close than when they sat farther away. The experience of being talked to at close range is captured by the authors' comment:

> The experimenters, who went through the procedure as subjects, found interaction at progressively closer distances to be a disquieting experience. As distance decreases, the speaker appears to focus his attention more intently upon the listener and gives the impression of trying to influence him. As a consequence it is difficult for the listener to relax. He must observe the social amenities of paying attention, reciprocating eye contact, and in general avoiding unnecessary movement. When he does engage

in expressive behavior, the listener tries to do so as unobtrusively as possible. (Albert & Dabbs, 1970, p. 269)

The major thrust of the findings in the studies we have described on interpersonal distance and social influence seems to indicate that close interpersonal distance is generally uncomfortable. The one exception is the Baron and Bell study. The conclusions regarding the effect of distance on persuasiveness are more confusing. Milgram (1965), Mehrabian and Williams (1969), and Baron and Bell (1976) obtained results which seem to indicate that proximity enhances influence. Yet the findings from the study by Albert and Dabbs (1970) would seem to indicate that proximity works against persuading people. It seems likely that the extent of the closeness, the duration of such approaches, and the content of the exchange, among other factors, may contribute to these contrasting results.

INFLUENCE AND OTHER NONVERBAL BEHAVIORS

Touch

The belief that touch is a medium of influence has a long and ancient history in religion and medicine. It is beyond the focus of this book to go into the rich lore surrounding the laying on of hands as a healing technique, but this form of nonverbal influence has been practiced by medico-religious persons for many centuries and in many diverse cultures.

In recent years there have been attempts to test the efficacy of touch in healing, with positive results (Grad, Cadoret, & Paul, 1961; Krieger, 1975), but it will take many studies with supportive findings before such a belief gains wide acceptance. Healing by touch shares with extrasensory perception both an air of mystery and low regard by the scientific community. However, one could more easily find psychological and physiological explanations of healing by touch than similar explanations for some of the extrasensory perception phenomena.

Touch has been found to have two general kinds of influences on people. First, in the right kind of setting touch is able to make people feel more positively about both external stimuli (Fisher, Rytting, & Heslin, 1976; Silverthorne, Noreen, Hunt, & Rota, 1972) and the toucher (Fisher et al., 1976). Second, in the right setting touch seems able to help recipients talk to other people, especially about themselves (Aguilera, 1967; Pattison, 1973). There is also some evidence that touching facilitates at least one form of influence: when people were asked to perform a favor (e.g., return money found in a phone booth), they were more likely to do so if the requester had touched them on the arm first before asking them for the money (Kleinke, 1977; 1980). Similarly, Willis and Hamm (1980) found more people signed a petition when they were touched (81%) by the requester than when they were not touched (55%), and more filled out a rating scale when touched (70%) than not touched (40%).

Facial Expression

One would expect the role of facial expression in social influence to be large, since the face is so visible and so variable in expression. Yet, there has not been as much research on facial expression and influence as such a large role would imply, and although it is not clear why there hasn't, we can propose two possible explanations. First, the face is so very visible that information about its role in social influence is already known and considered to be uninteresting. A second possible explanation is that the very complexity and subtlety of facial expression, with its changing from moment to moment, makes research extremely difficult. We think that the second explanation is more likely to be true.

Having noted the relative lack of research, let us turn to examine what there is. In general, most such research tends to deal with perhaps the most basic categorization of facial expression—whether a person is smiling or not. Smiling has been found to influence the impression people form of one another along one of the primary communication source characteristics, his or her attractiveness. In a study in which people were shown slides of a woman either smiling or not, observers considered her to be more interpersonally attractive when she was shown smiling 70% of the time (McGinley, McGinley, & Nicholas, 1978). This effect of smiling on attractiveness has been shown to be responsive to pacing. That is, when a woman first frowned and looked around the room while playing with the ends of her hair and then later oriented directly and smiled and nodded at the young man with whom she was conversing, observers concluded that the man's attraction toward her would be higher than when she was consistently "warm" toward him all the time (Clore, Wiggins, & Itkin, 1975). Smiling has also been found to create a positive impression in a job-interviewing situation (Washburn & Hakel, 1973).

The above examples dealt with aspects more relevant to the question of how a communication source would be received as a function of a person's facial expressions. Now we want to turn to the question of whether facial expression has a role in actually influencing the behavior of another person. A study by Elman, Schulte, and Bukoff (1977) focused primarily on the influence of gazing on the behavior of another person. In trying to replicate and test the generality of earlier research that had found that people leave an area more quickly when they have been subjected to steady gaze, these researchers found that the addition of a smile to the gaze appeared to neutralize the effects of a stare alone.

Research indicates that smiling has the ability to elicit smiling in the recipient when people are talking (Duncan, Brunner, & Fiske, 1979), and that it elicits tips from customers in a cocktail lounge (Tidd & Lockard, 1978). The broader the smile, the more the tip.

As indicated earlier, Ekman and Friesen (1969a; 1974) have proposed that facial expression is used successfully to deceive others. In an attempt to extend that finding to perception of whether a person is deceiving when responding to factual questions, both truthfully and untruthfully, Littlepage and Pineault (1979) showed videotapes of facial and body shots of persons answering questions. Observers were most accurate in recognizing what the respondent was really doing when they looked at body shots of people giving dishonest answers, supporting Ekman and Friesen's hypotheses.

The possibility that the face may not be giving the best information to the receiver was underscored by an earlier study by Bugental, Love, and Gianetto (1971). These researchers found that although a father's smiling was associated with approving statements to his child, there was no relation between whether the mother was smiling and whether what she said was approving or disapproving of the child. But even if a mother's smile may not be related to what she says, that doesn't mean that women are not sensitive to variations in facial expression and other nonverbal behaviors. They have been found repeatedly to be better decoders than men (Noller, 1980; Zuckerman, Hall, DeFrank, & Rosenthal, 1976). Also, we must reaffirm the caveat that there are definite *cultural* differences in the use of facial expression (Ishii, 1973). Many of the conclusions drawn from research on North Americans may not apply to people of other cultures.

Nonverbal Feedback

The perspective used in this discussion of social influence and nonverbal behavior has been one focusing on the communicator as the influencing agent. However, it is also clear that the audience's nonverbal reactions to a communicator can affect the communicator. Further, the communicator's own behavior can influence his or her own internal reactions or judgments. In the latter case, the martial displays of military and paramilitary groups and the rituals of fraternal, secret, and other similar organizations are meant to affect the participants as much as the observers (if, indeed, there are any non-participating observers present).

The notion that people's nonverbal behavior can be not only a manifestation of their internal state or a release of internal tension but also something capable of influencing the individuals themselves has been investigated by having people either exaggerate or minimize pain cues while being shocked (Lanzetta, Cartwright-Smith, & Kleck, 1976). These authors found that exaggerating and minimizing behaviors affect not only the person's reports of the painfulness of the shocks but also the actual autonomic response to the shocks. The major inference to be drawn from such a finding is that one of the strongest kinds of influence being mediated by nonverbal behavior has been relatively unnoticed: it is the influence that is being wrought directly on the behaving person. We would be derelict if we did not point out that there is also evidence that people who are very expressive behaviorally have been found to be *least* reactive physiologically. Based on this kind of research Buck (1980) has called into question the strength and generality of the facial-feedback model which the Lanzetta *et al.* (1976) study supports.

Appearance

People form impressions of each other from the moment they meet. Appearance is both the first information we get and a continuing influence on us. Even when another person stops talking and gesturing, his or her appearance is still constantly present. The question of interest to us is: Does appearance affect a person's credibility and ability to change another's attitude?

(Slim women and muscular men fit the stereotype of attractiveness for our culture and based on initial judgments, highest credibility ratings have been found to be given to female ectomorphs (slim build) and male mesomorphs)(muscular build) (Toomb & Divers, 1972). Of course, attractiveness judgments are influenced by other things besides physical build(For one half of a study population an attractive female confederate was made up (or down) to have an oily complexion, a trace of mustache on her lip, messy, loose-fitting clothing, and a noticeable absence of makeup. For the other half of the subjects she appeared as her normally attractive self. In addition to the two attractiveness levels, she indicated to the group in one condition that she was interested in influencing them and in another condition that she was not interested in influencing them. The authors found that when she indicated a desire to influence, male students changed their attitude in the direction of the position held by her when she appeared attractive more than when she appeared unattractive (Mills & Aronson, 1965).

Other examples of how attractiveness can increase a person's ability to influence someone else are given in a number of studies. For part of the study a female experimenter was made unattractive by the use of an unbecoming wig and an absence of all makeup; for the other part her appearance was left in its normal attractive state. During the course of the study she gave the male subjects a negative evaluation (shallow, immature, probably not creative, lacking in insight), or positive evaluation (earnest, reasonable, mature, well adjusted, frank, etc.). At the end of the experiment the subjects answered a number of questions, one of which was a rating of their liking for the female experimental assistant. If she was unattractive, her evaluation of the male subjects in either direction made no difference and the subjects' liking for her was at about the level of their feeling for the attractive experimenter who had given a negative evaluation. If she was attractive, the subjects liked her significantly more if she gave them a positive evaluation (Sigall & Aronson, 1969). Apparently a woman's power to influence men is significantly enhanced if she is attractive.

Even more relevant to the question of influence is a second study by Sigall (Sigall, Page, & Brown, 1969), in which an attractive or unattractive female experimenter gave either positive or negative feedback to male subjects on their performance on a standard athletic hand exerciser. She then told them that performance with the exerciser was a measure not only of strength but also of endurance and will, and she asked each one to retake the handgrip test. Table 3 indicates the difference between the first and second trials on the handgrip task. It shows difference in both the number of closures of the handgrip (Completions) and the total time worked (Time). The most noticeable result in Table 3 is that the subject worked less for the unattractive experimenter on the second try than he had on the first try for her male assistant (an average of 2.8 fewer squeezes when she had praised them and 1.2 fewer squeezes when she had told them that they had performed poorly the first time) and the attractive experimenter obtained more effort. Subjects also exerted greater effort after a negative evaluation of the first performance than after a positive evaluation. But the greatest differential in effort between positive and negative evaluation occurred when it was given by an attractive woman. Again, the evidence would seem to indicate that attractiveness in a woman definitely increases her power to influence men.

Physical attractiveness has an influence on credibility ratings also, but it does not influence all three components of credibility (trust-

Table 3. Mean Differences (T_2-T_1) in Number of Completed Squeezes and Working Time (in seconds)[a]

Group	Completions	Time
Attractive-positive	3.0	1.1
Unattractive-positive	−2.8	−8.0
Attractive-negative	7.8	15.3
Unattractive-negative	−1.2	−5.6

[a] Sigall, Page, & Brown, 1969, pp. 355–356.

worthiness, competence, and dynamism). When photographs of attractive and unattractive males and females were shown to male and
female subjects and they were asked to rate them on semantic-differential scales that measured the three components of credibility,
attractive photographs were rated significantly higher on "safety"
(trustworthiness) and on dynamism. Attractive people were not seen
as significantly higher on "qualification" (competence). Finally, there
was a tendency for males to see attractive people as more competent,
and females to see them as less competent (Widgery, 1974). More
recent research has confirmed that attractive sources are seen as more
interesting, warm, and so forth (Maddux & Rogers, 1980). But as far
as influence is concerned, some have found it to be facilitative (Chaiken, 1979), while others have found it to have no effect (Maddux &
Rogers, 1980).

   Although attractiveness is important, there are other aspects of
appearance that affect one person's influence over another, such as
how similar in appearance the two people are. For example, a petitioner soliciting signatures from peace demonstrators was more successful when he was dressed similarly to the demonstrators (Suedfeld,
Bochner, & Matas, 1971), people borrowing money for a telephone
call received more help from others who were similar to them in
whether they were dressed "straight" or "hippie" (Emswiller, Deaux,
& Willits, 1971), and political workers have greater success when they
are perceived as similar in attitude as denoted by choice of clothing
(Darley & Cooper, 1972).

   A sensitive area in which differences in appearance tends to be
heavily charged with emotion is hair length and beards. Knapp (1972)
recounts a news item from the May 11, 1970 issue of the *Milwaukee
Journal* that underscores the role of hair.

> Prof. William Larsen has a two-pound coffee can full of hair sacrificed by
> himself and about 30 young men attempting to bridge the generation
> gap. . . . He said stereotypes based on the way people look were so
> strongly ingrained that effective communication was impossible. Feelings
> about hair are as strong as on almost any subject, he said. (p. 78)

Research confirms Professor Larsen's intuition that hair has an impact
(Kenny & Fletcher, 1973). In one study, similar hairstyle produced
higher credibility between subjects. But they also found that bearded
males were perceived as more credible—a bit of a departure from

Professor Larsen's experience. Toomb and Repinsky (1973) report that with students, credibility was greater when the source had short hair and was well dressed.

Clothes can give force and credibility to one's words. In *The Prince and the Pauper*, Mark Twain (1881/1909, p. 18) describes a scene in which the Prince of Wales rushes out to reprimand a soldier for hitting the pauper who looks exactly like him. The prince pays no heed to the fact that he is still wearing the pauper's clothes after exchanging with him so each could experience vicariously what it must be to live the life of the other.

> The soldier that had maltreated Tom obeyed the prince's order to unbar the gate promptly; and as the prince burst through the portal, half smothered with royal wrath, the soldier fetched him a sounding box on the ear that sent him whirling to the roadway. . . .
>
> The prince picked himself out of the mud and made fiercely at the sentry, shouting, "I am the Prince of Wales, my person is sacred; and thou shalt hang for laying thy hand upon me!"
>
> The soldier . . . said . . . angrily, "Be off, thou crazy rubbish!"

There is evidence, albeit of a more prosaic nature, to support this notion of the importance of dress. Bickman (1974) has found that better dressed persons or a uniformed guard have more credibility than a milkman or civilian.

As we have seen in the case of the effect of appearance on liking, the effect of appearance on credibility may be strongest at initial encounters and less important as the recipient gets to know the person and hears what he or she has to say. For example, studies by Grantham (1973) and Hendrick, Stikes, and Murray (1972) found that the effect of race has little influence on credibility when observers have other information about the source.

What then can be concluded about the role of physical appearance on social influence? Clearly it would be overstating the case to imply that it is all important, but the evidence described above does indicate that it has an impact on whether a person is viewed as believable and able to get people to change their minds. Both absolute characteristics (attractiveness, uniform, etc.) and similarity in characteristics (hair, beard, dress) affect people's response. Thus, there appear to be four categories of reasons that appearance affects ability to persuade others. They are: (1) attractiveness, as a characteristic that makes people desirous of pleasing the person; (2) status indicators, as a sign that the person may have means–ends power over others; (3) similarity in appearance, as a sign that the person has a similar world view, needs, and experiences; and (4) signs (uniforms, etc.) that the person has expertise in the area under consideration.

Sex Differences

There appeared to be a pattern of findings running through a number of studies that was not seen by the authors of each study. The pattern seems to indicate that for women to be persuasive or to be taken as credible by an audience, they have to appear and present themselves as more serious and involved than do men. That conclusion is based on such findings as Mehrabian and Williams (1969) that when women were trying to be highly persuasive, they swiveled less than either men in general or women when they were not trying to be persuasive. Furthermore, men were viewed as more persuasive when their shoulder orientation was indirect rather than direct, while for women the opposite tended to be true. Similarly, women were perceived as being less persuasive and men more persuasive the more relaxed their body posture.

The implication of these findings is that men have to mute their attention-gaining power and women have to augment theirs for optimum persuasiveness. Similar findings were also obtained by Mehrabian and Williams on the effect of moderate or high gaze on perceived persuasiveness. When they became more intense by gazing 90% of the time, men lost persuasiveness but women gained persuasiveness. Again, it seems that women have to try harder to get the serious attention of people. Women in persuasive roles (Congress, women's rights, etc.) have been unjustly accused of being strident and having personality problems. If a woman wants to make a point and she is having difficulty being taken seriously, she is in a double bind. If she wishes to compensate for a poor audience response she will have to make her nonverbal behavior more immediate and intense. But if she does that, the same audience will accuse her of being strident.

Nonverbal Behavior and the Regulation of Everyday Life

One of the major tasks of any system of interpersonal relations is to insure that people conduct their interpersonal affairs with a minimum of embarrassment and discomfort. When two people meet, whether for business or pleasure, they are guided both by a shared sense of what is expected in that kind of situation and by the cues emitted by the other person. The behavior of the other person is a necessary clue to exactly how to behave because there is some latitude allowed in the interpretation of any situation. Thus, closing a business deal can be either a "strictly business" transaction or a friendly business one.

Nonverbal behavior is involved, therefore, in regulating the degree of intimacy between participants by signaling the degree of involvement each person is ready to commit to the transaction. The first event in an encounter is usually some form of greeting. There are a number of subtle and not-so-subtle differences in how one executes a greeting, depending on socially relevant characteristics, such as the person's cultural background (the Lebanese greet differently than the Japanese), sex, age, or relationship (Heslin & Boss, 1980).

As the conversation develops, nonverbal behavior serves a quite different function. It is important in assuring that the transition between speaker and listener roles proceeds smoothly, without simultaneous speaking and without the long pauses caused by one person not knowing whether the other person has finished speaking. At one level, nonverbal cues such as looking and nodding may facilitate the flow of conversation, but they also give clues about the future direction of that interaction. In this chapter we will not be discussing the detailed and complex function of nonverbal cues in conversational sequencing. While this is an important and interesting issue, our concerns here will focus on the more general issue of regulating the initiation, development, and termination of interactions. The reader interested in the problem of conversational sequencing *per se* should examine the excellent reviews by Rosenfeld (1978) and Feldstein and Welkowitz (1978).

Perhaps the greatest function of nonverbal behavior is that it allows foreshadowing or partial communication of matters that might be demeaning or offensive if actually verbalized. When social relations are moving smoothly, people do not need to ask many questions about the interaction itself. The glances, the tone of voice, body lean, length of response, and facial expression usually provide sufficient evidence about the other person to permit a reasonable reading of his or her intentions or desires.

Nonverbal cues also allow the person to maintain privacy from encroachment by unwanted others (Altman, 1975). One of the informal controls that seems to be going on continuously in interpersonal interaction is the movement toward and away from people so as to result in maximizing our satisfaction with social exchange. Relative status differences between interactants are often critical in determining what kinds of interactions will be sought and how different interactions are managed. Usually, the closer two persons are in status the more comfortable they will be, at least in casual, noncompetitive exchanges. Once the interaction is initiated, the higher-status person usually takes the lead in deciding whether the relationship will continue or not because he or she usually has less to gain from the relationship. This status equilibrium process works best at the nonverbal level. In fact, we are so used to taking and receiving cues nonverbally, that we find it difficult to handle properly those situations in which the other person ignores the relevant nonverbal cues. For example, it is embarrassing and irritating to have to tell someone we do not want to listen to him or her anymore. Most of the time, the other person recognizes from our behavior that we are bored or impatient, and that person terminates the interaction. The bore does not. Neither does the boorish salesman who uses norms about cues in conversation to his own purpose. We are forced to verbalize what should not need to be verbalized: "Please, I really do not want any of them!"

Thus the nonverbal behavior accompanies and regulates the easy flow of conversation, both at the mechanical level of conversational sequencing and at the interpersonal evaluational level. The conversation progresses and so does the relationship, often at a level that would be invisible to a person who might later examine a transcript of what was said. Comparable verbal content on topics such as the weather, gossip of the day, or business matters may be common to qualitatively very different experiences in two contrasting interactions. In such cases the nonverbal exchange clearly sets the tone for the interaction.

At some point, the conversation (or even the relationship) comes to an end or is redefined. Again, nonverbal behavior plays a role in signaling that it is time to terminate, so that both persons can avoid the appearance that one person is leaving the other. Let us now go through the components of social interaction in more detail than above, looking at the way in which nonverbal behavior facilitates social-regulatory processes at each phase.

GREETING

Most of the time when people pass on the street or in halls, they grant each other what is referred to as "civil inattention" (Goffman, 1963). This involves looking away from other persons when you approach within 10 to 15 feet of them. Scheflen (1972) breaks Goffman's term down into two parts. First the people glance at each other from time to time up to about 15 feet. This is being "civil" and recognizing the presence of the other person. Closer than about 15 feet, they avert their eyes as they pass. This is the "inattention" part and grants to the other person his or her privacy. Continuing to look within 15 feet, the distance usually given to inattention, can be interpreted as conveying either a challenge (Ellsworth, Carlsmith, & Henson, 1972) or an invitation, depending on the situation and the person's facial expression. Ignoring the other person totally, including the distance beyond the range for inattention, might signal rejection. While Goffman's and Scheflen's descriptions have a ring of truth to them, at least one study failed to support their observations. Specifically, in a series of studies of passing pedestrians, Cary (1978) found no evidence of the gaze patterns described by Goffman and Scheflen. While Cary's results might be interpreted as refuting Goffman and Scheflen, it is also possible that additional factors such as sidewalk density, setting, or characteristics of the subjects could account for this failure to support their theorizing.

The circumstance of passing another person whom we may have met but would not consider a friend provides an interesting instance for examination. When we pass such a person we have to decide whether or not we wish to acknowledge the relationship. One way such an acknowledgement is conveyed is through an "eyebrow flash"— a rapid elevation of the eyebrows usually accompanied by a raising of the head. Eibl-Eibesfeldt (1972) has observed the eyebrow flash in a variety of cultures as a component of greeting. If mutual eyebrow flashes do not occur, the two people usually pass one another without further involvement. If an apparent stranger gives an eyebrow flash to someone, the recipient is likely to wonder how or where the stranger knew him.

In one detailed study of greeting patterns, the researchers filmed people arriving at an outdoor birthday party (Kendon & Ferber, 1973). They found that there was a period of mutual gaze and a distant salutation initially when the host and guest were first seeing each other "officially." Then while the guest was getting close enough for a close salutation she averted her gaze, groomed herself, and freed her right hand. The host and guest looked at each other just before shaking hands or embracing. When guests looked at each other, there was not the moving together as had occurred with the host unless there was a relatively clear indication of desire to do so by one of the persons. Such an interest might be signaled by a prolonged gaze or reorientation toward that person. The probability of initiating or reciprocating greetings is undoubtedly a product of numerous factors such as personality differences, the nature of the setting, and the relationship between individuals.

Given that a greeting will be exchanged in some fashion, there are the additional concerns of both the level and amount of the greeting exchange. Berne (1972) refers to this kind of interchange as mutual stroking. Some greetings are one-stroke interchanges, while others may be five-stroke interchanges. An example of a one-stroke exchange is "Morning, Charles," "Morning, Fred." An example of a two-stroke interchange is "Morning, Charles," "Morning, Fred," "Nice day," "Sure is." Concern may arise when the strokes do not balance. It is as if people have two goals. First, most people would like to have the number of strokes exchanged be at a level appropriate to their intended degree of involvement with the other person. Second, they would like whatever number of strokes they give to be reciprocated, no more and no less. We said that the setting and the relationship between the persons who are greeting affect how they greet.

Heslin and Boss (1980) conducted a study designed to examine nonverbal immediacy as it occurred spontaneously in a natural setting. Setting was not varied. Instead an airport was chosen as an obvious setting, and attention was focused on the greeting and departure rituals there.

The study was based on certain hypotheses. First, psychological closeness (friendship, etc.) relates to propinquity; that is, a traveler is more likely to be met or sent off by someone with whom she or he has an intimate relationship. Second, the closeness of a relationship is positively related to the intimacy of greeting. Finally, touching is initiated more often by males than females in cross-sex pairs and by older persons in cross-age pairs.

Travelers and randomly chosen persons from among the people who had come to meet or send them off were observed and queried about their relationship.

Intimacy of Actual Encounter

From the 10 individual types of touch observed, an intimacy scale of six levels was developed based on the intimacy of the combination of touches observed in each pair.

0. No touch
1. Handshake, or touched on head, arm, or back
2. Light hug, or arm around waist or back, or held hand, or kiss on cheek, or two from 1 above

3. Solid hug, or kiss on mouth, or three from 1 and 2 above
4. Extended embrace, both kiss on mouth and solid hug, or either kiss on mouth or solid hug and two from 1 and 2 above
5. Extended kiss, or extended embrace plus kiss on mouth, or extended embrace plus solid hug plus any other, or four or more of any category above 2

The six intimacy levels of actual encounter occurred with the following frequency: 0 = 16%, 1 = 12%, 2 = 16%, 3 = 28%, 4 = 11%, and 5 = 18%. Categories 0 and 1 would have had higher frequencies if there had been strangers in the sample.

At the most primitive level of interpersonal distance is the question of merely being present when a traveler leaves or returns. The intimacy of the relationship between the traveler and the person selected from his or her greeting or send-off group was positively related to the frequency of occurrence in the sample. The closeness of the relationship between the two persons also showed a solid correlation with intimacy of encounter.

Thus, both the choice to be in the presence of another person and the intimacy of greeting toward that person were congruent with the closeness of their relationship. Such congruence between kinds of closeness represents a different aspect of equilibrium theory (Argyle & Dean, 1965) than has usually been emphasized.

There was a nonsignificant tendency for males to initiate touching more than females in cross-sex pairs and significantly more older than younger people initiated touch in cross-sex encounters but not in the same-sex encounters. These results lent weak support to Goffman's (1967) proposal that higher-status persons have greater freedom to initiate touch with lower-status persons than vice versa, and less support to Henley's (1973) proposal that males, having higher status, have greater freedom to initiate touch with females.

However, it is also possible that the data are a result of distaste on the part of the females and younger people rather than the power of the initiator. The fact that in same-sex pairs older people did not initiate touch more than younger people weakens the status interpretation and supports the proposal that recipients may be manifesting lower attraction than the initiator in a situation where attraction is a consideration—in cross-sex interactions.

Table 4. Tactile Involvement between Traveler and Other

No touch[a]	41[b]	Holding hands	12
Handshake	10	Kiss on cheek	30
Touch on head, arm, back	38	Solid hug	19
Light hug	23	Kiss on mouth	41
Arm around waist or back	15	Extended embrace	10
		Extended kiss	3

[a] Contact categories in order of increasing intimacy.
[b] Refers to the number of dyads (from a total of 103) that engaged in that behavior. The total number of touches is greater than 103 because many dyads engaged in more than one kind of touch.

In the same-sex interaction, pairs of women gave and received more solid hugs, scored higher on the touch intimacy scale, engaged in more frequent contact, and touched each other on the head, arm, or back more than pairs of men. Pairs of men shook hands more than pairs of women.

Touching *per se* was moderately high, with 60% of the dyads touching in at least some way. When this is compared with Jourard's (1966) and Henley's (1973) American norm of 2 touches per hour, it is clear that arrival and departure rituals are favorable settings for the study of naturally occurring touch. Another recent study of greeting behavior at the airport (Greenbaum & Rosenfeld, 1980) supports such a view, with even a higher percentage (83%) of dyads engaging in some kind of contact.

However, as can be seen in Table 4, there is a general tendency for the more intimate kinds of touch to be relatively infrequent. The most severe departures from a monotonic relationship seemed to be a handshake, which occurred less often, and kiss on the mouth, which occurred more often than such a relationship might predict.

In conclusion, the Heslin and Boss (1980) results supported the hypothesis that the intimacy of a relationship would predict the level of nonverbal involvement manifested.

ACCESS

Access operates at two levels. The first level deals with whether a person has given permission to another to begin a conversation. A person begins a request from a stranger with an "Excuse me," indicating awareness that the privacy buffer of the other person has been violated. In fact, touching people (Sussman & Rosenfeld, 1978), sitting by them (Sommer, 1969; Quick & Crano, 1973), or lying next to them at a swimming pool (Quick & Crano, 1973), if done without invitation or explanation, yields negative reactions, especially from males. As Figure 5 shows, gazing without relating can be viewed as intrusive. However, friendliness of an invader can affect how he or she is received (Storms & Thomas, 1977; Quick & Crano, 1973).

The second level of access signaling continues during interaction and indicates accessibility regarding future engagements and, indeed, the expected length and intensity of the present meeting. A number of access signals have similarity to courtship signals, and Scheflen (1965) has referred to these as "quasi-courtship behaviors." They include four categories of behavior. The first category includes such things as improved muscle tonus, reduced eye bagginess and jowl sag, lessening of shoulder hunching and slouch, and decreasing belly sag, all of which he refers to as *courtship readiness*. The second category is *preening behavior* and is characterized by stroking the hair, adjusting one's clothing, glancing in the mirror, and touching up makeup. The third category is *positional cues*, which involve orienting one's shoulders, torso, and arms so as to form a closed group, one that says "We are not open to intrusion right now." Finally, there are *actions of appeal or invitation*, which include gestures of interest, such as holding the other person's gaze, and flirtation, such as looking out of the corner of the eye coupled with a half smile, pouting mouth, exhibiting wrist and palm, crossing legs to expose a thigh, rolling of the hips, and so on.

Scheflen contends that much of normal interaction contains some elements that have courtship characteristics, even when courtship is not a consideration, such as a conversation between two heterosexual males or even exchanges in psychotherapy. It appears to us that the components in common are those in the first and third category— those that indicate involvement and interest in relating to the other person, and that relate to making a good impression on the other person. These convey access and indicate to the other person that he or she is free to continue and deepen the interaction and relationship.

The control of access can be accomplished in ways that are indirect. One technique that is being examined is through the use of

Figure 5. Negative response to gaze. Copyright, 1977, G.B. Trudeau. Reprinted with permission of Universal Press Syndicated. All rights reserved.

telecommunication. Although apparently less immediate than face-to-face interaction, communication by telephone, videophone, and even by letter can intrude and "crowd" someone (Kaplan & Greenberg, 1976) in the sense of forcing one's presence on another person.

One can adjust future accessibility merely by the way in which statements are couched. "One of these days we should get together." "We should get together next week." "Perhaps we can have lunch next week." "Lunch at the Peking next Tuesday!" Clearly these sentences vary in the degree that they evidence polite distancing or hesitancy, with the last one being the most definite and immediate (Wiener & Mehrabian, 1968).

There are some who believe that it is clever to give the impression that access to them is not readily attainable. They hope that they convey the impression that they are "special," "unattainable," "rare," "not common." Often they attempt to convey low access by acting aloof or distant. Whether such a technique works depends on a number of factors, but it has had a long history as indicated by the fact that it was recommended by Socrates to the prostitute Theodota:

> SOCRATES: They will appreciate your favors most highly if you wait till they ask for them. The sweetest meats, you see, if served before they are wanted seem sour, and to those who have had enough they are positively nauseating; but even poor fare is very welcome when offered to a hungry man.
>
> THEODOTA: And how can I make them hungry for my fare?
>
> SOCRATES: Why, in the first place, you must not offer it to them when they have had enough—but prompt them by behaving as a model of propriety, by a show of reluctance to yield, and by holding back until they are as keen as can be; and then the same gifts are much more to the recipient than when they're offered before they are desired. (Xenophon, 1923, p. 48)

Using reduced personal accessibility to enhance attractiveness has been brought under scientific scrutiny in a series of studies by Walster, Walster, Piliavin, and Schmidt (1973). In the first study, when males in a computer-dating situation called the number given to them, they heard either a female who eagerly accepted their offer or one who played hard-to-get. When playing hard-to-get, she indicated that she had met a lot of people since signing up for the computer-dating service and was pretty busy all week. After some hesitation, she agreed to go on the date with the subject. After the dates, subjects were contacted and asked to evaluate their date. Whether or not the girl played hard-to-get did not affect the ratings given to her.

In their second study, Walster *et al.* enlisted the assistance of a prostitute. She told a portion of her customers that she would be busy in the future so that even if she saw them this time, that was not a guarantee that she would be able to see them in the future. The men toward whom she played hard-to-get liked her less than those toward whom she acted normally.

Thus the first two studies do not support the notion that playing hard-to-get increases a person's attractiveness. Interviews of men indicated that playing hard-to-get by women causes men to feel anxious and have doubts about their acceptability. This response may be at least partially sex-specific; other findings indicate that men are more liked when they are distant and mysterious, but women are more liked when they are open and disclosing (Chelune, 1976). In order to pursue the possibility that playing hard-to-get threatened the self-esteem of the men, Walster *et al.* conducted a third study.

In the third study, there were three groups of women: those who gave evidence of easy availability for all men, those who presented themselves as hard-to-get for all men, and those who indicated that they were hard-to-get for most men but not for the caller. The third group of women—who evidenced high selectivity in general but high acceptance of the subject—were most liked by a large factor. They seemed to be both popular and yet easy to get along with.

In controlling one's accessibility, one can be aware or unaware, discreet or clumsy, discriminating or indiscriminate. Although the confederates in the Walster study conveyed access information directly and verbally, such an overt technique was necessary for purposes of experimental control and is probably less the rule than is the use of nonverbal indices of access. One conveys one's enthusiasm facially, with voice tone, body orientation, interpersonal distance, and in a myriad of subtle ways during an ongoing conversation.

One situation in which we have all regulated our accessibility is in the classroom. The hand raised by a student is an overt "emblem" (Ekman & Friesen, 1969), which has the clearly understood meaning (especially in this setting) of desire to communicate. We may be less aware that we are communicating when we lean forward and show other signs of interest. Controlling accessibility at a level that may or may not be out of awareness are behaviors such as whether a student attends class on a given day, where he or she sits, how the teacher arranges the seats or desks, whether a rostrum is used, and so on. Thus we have four situations involving nonverbal behavior. They are:

1. Behaviors which the actor initiates because he or she means to communicate something to the recipient and both persons know it
2. Behaviors of the actor's that are meant to communicate something to the recipient but done in such a way that the recipient is not sure whether it was intended
3. Behaviors which are probably not meant to communicate but which do reflect an attitude or feeling of the actor
4. Behaviors which are probably not meant to communicate and which may not even reflect an attitude or feeling of the actor

Someone else's tardiness is an example of behavior that can be classified in Category 2, 3, or 4. To what do you ascribe it? To hostility? To thoughtlessness? To obstacles beyond the actor's control? The relevant and appropriate decision for such a nonverbal manifestation is that "more information is needed."

A Category 3 behavioral situation that is relevant to the question of access is reduced eye contact by the student in a classroom (Knapp, 1972). When the teacher asks a question and then glances across the room to call on someone, those who do not know the answer look down or out the window. The one place they do not look is at the teacher, because eye contact gives the teacher access to the student.

It is the same when the restaurant customer tries to catch the eye of the waiter who is busy with other things. Access to the waiter is denied to the customer. For those waiters who make it their business never to be too busy with other things to see a request for service from a customer, we would like to see a generous 25 to 35% tip. For those whose eyes are averted most of the time, no tip!

STATUS

One of the functions (if not the most important function) of social-regulatory processes is the maintenance of the status hierarchy. To-day, there is less of an income differential between blue-collar and white-collar workers than there used to be, and the graduated income tax has further reduced the difference in take-home pay. So what are the ways in which we reward those who seem to contribute more to society or whose abilities are in shorter supply? One can still see some of the trappings of status, especially at the very top of governmental and corporate power. These include chauffeur-driven limousines, spacious secluded offices, use of the company's airplane or first-class accommodations on commercial flights, and large expense accounts. Henley (1977) has detailed a number of such privileges for those in high places.

One perquisite of status that has yet to be thoroughly studied is the use of time, one of the most sensitive indices of power. Henley (1977) draws a parallel between E. T. Hall's (1966) four levels of spatial intimacy (intimate, personal, social, and public) and time allocation.

For encounters with *public* figures, time allotted approaches zero. That is, very few people get to talk to them at all; some get to shake their hand; most get nothing. Encounter at the *social* level can range from a few moments up to around 15 minutes. The typical social encounter is a business transaction. The *personal* encounter usually takes from 15 to 30 minutes. These include counseling sessions and other appointments, for example, with physicians and dentists, which place the personal encounter at a level more intimate than purchasing something at a store but less intimate than a conversation with a friend. The *intimate* encounter generally involves more than 30 minutes. Intimate encounters range from therapy sessions, marriage counseling, and so on at the short time end to dating and marriage at the long time end of the intimate zone. Henley also proposes that there is a time limit even at the very intimate level for most people that is around a few hours. That is, uninterrupted intimacy with someone beyond 2 to 3 hours starts to become tedious to at least one of the persons.

Keeping other people waiting is a manifestation of status and enhances the value of the higher status person and his or her service. For example the longer it took a business executive to answer a knock on the door, the more status was ascribed to him by observers (Burns, 1964). Patients often remain in a doctor's waiting room for a half hour or more before being ushered into the examination room. There they may wait for another considerable period before the physician arrives.

The phrase "Let him cool his heels for a while" reflects the view that having to wait is punishing and "making them wait" is a prerogative of the privileged.

Higher-status people seldom wait, have more freedom of movement (Esser, Chamberlain, Chapple, & Kline, 1965), have larger spaces around them, have more aesthetically pleasing environments, use the words and paralinguistic accompaniments of power and freedom (casual use of language), are free to touch others, look where and as long as they wish, and smile when and only when they are amused. Lower-status persons and women do not enjoy these privileges as much as higher-status persons and men (Firestone, 1970; Henley, 1977).

An example of such rights is given by Goffman (1967):

> At staff meetings on the psychiatric units of the hospital, medical doctors had the privilege of swearing, changing the topic of conversation, and sitting in undignified positions; attendants, on the other hand, had the right to attend staff meetings and to ask questions during them . . . but were implicitly expected to conduct themselves with greater circumspection than was required of doctors. . . . Similarly, doctors had the right to saunter into the nurses' station, lounge on the station's dispensing counter, and engage in joking with the nurses; other ranks participated in this informal interaction with doctors, but only after doctors had initiated it. (pp. 78–79)

In one study, the relation between status and invasive nonverbal behavior was investigated using a sociodrama-type setting. As one would expect from the proposals above, when touching was encouraged in role-playing situations, the person in the dominant role touched more often than did the person in the submissive role (Alber, 1974).

Status differences are apparent not only in general demeanor, but even in vocal characteristics. People were able to make inferences about the social class of another person based solely on their conversation in response to standardized questions and instructions (Harms, 1961). Listeners reported having made up their mind within the first 10 to 15 seconds of hearing the person's voice. In another study people who spoke standard English were given higher-status ratings than someone with a Mexican-American accent (Ryan & Carranza, 1975).

One of the least ambiguous articles on the role of the paralinguistic characteristics of a person's speech and his or her perceived social status is the classic study by Ellis (1967). He first had students make a 40-second recording of their version of Aesop's fable "The Tortoise and the Hare." Then listeners rated the speakers on social class. Their rating correlated ($r = +.80$) with the speaker's actual social class, regardless of regional accents.

Ellis next tried to remove the effect of grammar and diction by having a group of students play the role of upper-class students giving the university president and the president's guests a tour of a new dormitory. Even though all subjects used proper grammar, listeners' rankings of social status correlated ($r = +.65$) with actual social status.

In an attempt to remove other contextual cues, such as the length of the sentence used by the subject or the student's choice of vocabulary, a third study was conducted in which subjects had only to count from 1 to 20. Even with this greatly reduced context, listeners were able to estimate the social status of the speaker quite well ($r = +.65$).

Thus vocal characteristics are used with quite good accuracy to judge another person's social status. People can quickly draw conclusions about each other and proceed according to those conclusions without having to embarrass or insult each other.

Gazing is not related to social status as clearly as vocal characteristics. The lack of clarity concerning the relationship between gazing and social status results from gaze serving different, often contrasting functions. There are some reasons for gazing more at other persons with higher status, for example, to monitor their reactions to you, to admire them, and perhaps to challenge them. Reasons for gazing less in the presence of a higher-status person may include feeling less dominant, relaxed, and self-confident (Fugita, 1974). In contrast, the more dominant member of a pair has the prerogative to gaze either more or less at the subordinate member. Dominance hierarchies have been demonstrated in terms of who lowers his or her eyes first when each gazes at one another (Strongman & Champness, 1968). The whole relationship between gazing and dominance becomes further complicated because gazing can also serve to indicate sexual interest in another person (Henley, 1973).

Status can also affect gestures, posture, and other expressive behaviors. For example, people are more likely to put their hands on their hips (arms akimbo) and to manifest hand and foot relaxation when addressing a lower- (compared to a higher-) status person

(Mehrabian, 1969). Higher-status people are also expected to sit in special places, usually to occupy the "head" position (Lott & Sommer, 1967). The head of the family usually sits at the head of the table. People who chair meetings are expected to sit at the head of the table where they can see and be seen by the members. This very association of the end of a table with status is well enough known that people who are aware of their status may avoid the use of it in casual living situations (Heckle, 1973). But at more formal occasions, such as large banquets, the guests of honor do sit at the "head table."

Pellegrini (1971) found that the person who occupies the head position at a rectangular table rather than a side position is more likely to be rated higher on status and dominance. Similarly, Strodtbeck and Hook (1961) found that the people who sat at the head of the table were most likely to be picked for jury supervisor, especially if they were seen as being from a high socioeconomic class. But sitting at the head of a table is not a guarantee that you will have leadership characteristics ascribed to you. Researchers have found that participants of leaderless discussion groups are unaffected by seating arrangement in their ratings of each other on leadership (Bass & Klubeck, 1952). In general, when one moves from the laboratory to real-world situations the relationship between seating position at a table and perception of status is complicated by the very great likelihood that more dominant personalities will tend to pick end positions or avoid the corner positions of a table. Furthermore people in these end positions talk more than those in corner positions. Thus, it is difficult to determine the direction of causality but there is fairly good evidence that sitting at the head of a table and being seen as dominant are associated.

Status has been seen to affect the sheer distance people stand from each other. E. T. Hall cites an example given in Theodore White's *The Making of the President 1960*. The following event occurred after it became clear that Kennedy had the nomination.

> Kennedy loped into the cottage with his light, dancing step, as young and lithe as springtime, and called a greeting to those who stood in his way. Then he seemed to slip from them as he descended the steps of the split-level cottage to a corner where his brother Bobby and brother-in-law Sargent Shriver were chatting, waiting for him. The others in the room surged forward on impulse to join him. Then they halted. A distance of perhaps 30 feet separated them from him, but it was impassable. They

stood apart, these older men of long-established power, and watched him. He turned after a few minutes, saw them watching him, and whispered to his brother-in-law. Shriver now crossed the separating space to invite them over. First Averell Harriman; then Dick Daley; then Mike DiSalle, then one by one, let them all congratulate him. Yet no one could pass the little open distance between him and them uninvited, because there was this thin separation about him, and the knowledge they were there not as his patrons but as his clients. They could come by invitation only, for this might be a President of the United States. (E. T. Hall, 1966, pp. 124–125)

The effect of status on the distance around a person was investigated by having two people talk in a hallway at a distance that would allow people to walk between them. The higher-status conversers had fewer people walk between them than did lower-status conversers (Buckley, Lindskold, Wayner, & Albert, 1976; Knowles 1973). It has also been found that people will invade the space of low-status (offbeat) dyads more than high-status (straight) dyads (Walker & Borden, 1976). It looks as if "different from oneself" is not as important a judgment as "higher status" in causing a person to walk around others.

The distance that one person moves into the office of another apparently relates to status (Burns, 1964). If a caller stops just inside the door and converses from there, observers consistently rate the person as subordinate. Similarly, when investigators studied the relation between status and distance in the military (where the status of participants can be readily ascertained), they found that when people talked to a superior they stood farther away than when interacting with a peer, and that the greater the discrepancy between the status of the initiator and the superior, the greater the distance between them (Dean, Hewitt, & Willis, 1975). Other researchers have found that people sit closer to peers than to persons of higher or lower status (Lott & Sommer, 1967) and are more likely to flee following an invasion of their space by a higher-status invader than by a peer (Barash, 1973).

In general, the greater space, freedom, and time available to higher-status people should reduce the amount of stress they experience from distractions and overstimulation and from boredom and understimulation. Whatever the underlying dynamics, it seems clear that the higher-status or more dominant individual consistently has

greater control over his or her social accessibility than do less dominant individuals.

REGULATION IN CONVERSATION

When we use the phrase "social-regulatory processes" we are
referring to the general function of nonverbal behavior to regulate
privacy, status, intimacy, and the occurrence of social gaffes. But there
is a specific class of nonverbal behaviors that have been termed by
Ekman and Friesen (1969b) as "regulators." They are so named because they regulate the back-and-forth flow of conversation. They
consist of those behaviors relating to both the initiation and sequencing of, and reactions to, verbal interaction. Studying behaviors involved in conversational turn-taking or floor apportionment has utility
in evaluating the subtle responses to the interaction. For example,
Argyle, Lalljee, and Cook (1968) judged that "It looks as if males are
motivated to dominate and do so largely by interrupting and talking
more, especially when the normal cues for floor apportionment are
absent" (p. 15). Thorne and Henley (1975) cite studies in which husbands answer for their wives more than vice versa (Kester, 1972) and
males interrupt females more than the other way around (Zimmerman
& West, 1975).

One thing stands out in Table 5. There is a greater tendency for
people to look at the other person while listening (75%) than while

Table 5. Amount of Gaze in Dyads[a]

Gaze Measure	Sex Combination				
	MM[b]	FF	MF(M)	MF(F)	Average of all combinations
Total individual gaze (%)	56	66	66	54	61
Looking while listening (%)	74	78	76	69	75
Looking while talking (%)	31	48	52	36.5	41
Mutual gaze (%)	23	38	31.5		31
Length of individual glances (sec)	2.45	3.12	3.61	2.98	2.95
Length of mutual glances (sec)	.86	1.42	1.25		1.18

[a] Argyle and Ingham, 1972.
[b] MM means two males, FF means two females, MF(M) means a male as he relates to a female,
and MF(F) means a female as she relates to a male.

talking (41%). Two things contribute to the difference in looking between speakers and listeners. First, the speaker needs to be concentrating on his or her thoughts and not be distracted by the listener. Second, the speaker runs the risk of having to yield the floor before finishing his or her point if eye contact is made. However, the reason the speaker does not look away completely during a speaking turn is due to the speaker's need to monitor the listener's reactions.

Bakeman and Dabbs (1976) describe a new approach that facilitates gathering and analyzing behaviors that might occur in conversational sequences. Basically, the procedure for gathering data is to press a button whenever a behavior begins and press another button whenever it ends. A computer program uses a clock to calculate occurrence, duration, joint occurrence, and likelihood that certain events will precede other events. Figure 6 depicts results obtained when Bakeman and Dabbs coded talking and looking. We can see that the most common behavior was simply looking at the other person (.40). We can also see that previous behavior is the best predictor of future behavior, that is, the highest probability is that people will do next whatever they are doing now (.86, .71, .73, and .66). Furthermore, looking (.40 + .25 = .65) is more likely to occur than not looking (.21 + .15 = .36). The frequency of looking and talking (.25) plus talking only (.21) gives a probability of .46 for talking. From this we can calculate the probability of looking while talking as .65 × .46 = .30. That is, given that the average person spends 65% of the time looking at the other person and 46% of the time talking, the person should spend about 30% of the time looking while talking at the same time. The obtained proportion of .25 for looking while talking is close to the predicted proportion of .30.

The difference in looking while talking versus looking while listening is supportive of earlier research. For example, Nielsen (1962) found that 38% of the time the speaker was talking he or she was looking at the recipient, whereas the listener was looking fully 62% of the time. Nielsen also found that people differ considerably in how much they look at another person. In 10-minute conversations, for example, subjects varied greatly: some spent only 8% of their time looking at the other person (92% of their time looking somewhere else!) and others spent 73% of the time looking at the other person. However, it seems clear that patterns of gaze toward others manifest

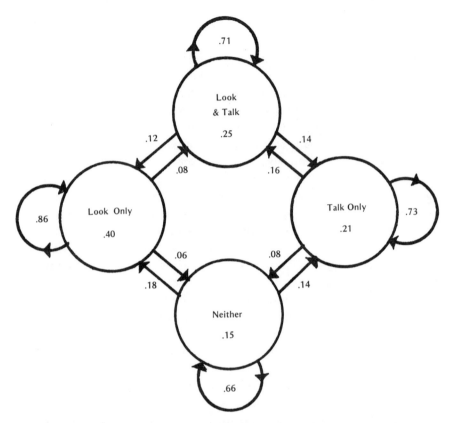

Figure 6. Mean patterns of talking and looking during conversation. Numbers represent simple and transitional probabilities among the four possible states within a subject, based upon observations every 1/2 second for 6 minutes on each of 66 subjects. Transitional probabilities smaller than .03 are not shown (Based on Bakeman & Dabbs, 1976).

high intraindividual stability over time (Daniell & Lewis, 1972; Patterson, 1973a). It is interesting that, on the average, people looked at the other person 50% of the time.

There are different ways of calculating what would be a reasonable expected amount of eye contact or mutual gaze; one approach (Strongman & Champness, 1968) would be simply to multiply the amount that *A* looks at *B* times the amount of time that *B* looks at *A* (similar to calculating the probability of the joint occurrence of *A* and *B* as the product of the probability of each occurring by itself). Argyle and Cook (1976) have an interesting discussion of both the Strongman and Champness approach and a modification proposed by Argyle and Ingham (1972). The latter proposal takes into account the fact that people look more when listening and less when talking. Because the most frequent looking times for each person may be out of phase with the other person, the straight multiplication to estimate the probability of mutual gaze by the Strongman and Champness approach may overestimate the amount of mutual gaze. This issue is still being investigated.

For an interaction to proceed smoothly, there needs to be some degree of coordination on a number of aspects of the interaction. There must be agreement about: (1) the content of the interaction, (2) the role relationships (e.g., who is teacher and who is pupil), (3) the level of intimacy, (4) the dominance relationship, (5) the emotional tone of the interaction (e.g., are they joking or serious?), and (6) the approximate length of time the interaction will take. They also must (1) time and synchronize their speaking, (2) sequence their behavior appropriately (questions are followed by answers, etc.), and (3) respond nonverbally to each other. The cues to help coordinate these behaviors, especially the timing and synchronizing of speech, have been studied by Kendon (1967) and others (e.g., Duncan, 1972; Kendon, 1972; Levine & Sutton-Smith, 1973; Weisbrod, 1967). By detailed analysis of films, Kendon (1967) showed how people take turns speaking (floor apportionment) and signal when they want it or do not want it.

In addition to the tendency for someone to look less when talking than listening, which we discussed above, Kendon noted that speakers look at listeners when they finish their major point. At this time, the listeners, who have been gazing more or less steadfastly at the speakers, look away as they start to speak. If speakers wish to hold onto the floor they can pick up their pace vocally, so that the pause is not long enough for easy entry, or fill the gap with sound ("um," "uh"). They can also raise one finger to indicate a point to come or raise their hand, palm outward, to indicate that the other person should not begin or should stop trying to interrupt. These last gestures are often made by the speaker even while he or she is looking away. During the conversation listeners nod or say "uh-huh" to let the speaker know that they are listening and understanding what is being said (Argyle, 1969, p. 202). Such responses by a listener can serve as reinforcers and are usually not considered to be discrete turns in speaking; they are listener responses, not a speaker's turn.

One means by which individuals facilitate their talk is by setting a matching pace. Thus, they move toward similarity in length of utterance (Matarazzo, Wiens, & Saslow, 1965), length of pause (Argyle & Kendon, 1967), the use of certain words such as "I," "you," and "the," amount of self-disclosure (Taylor, 1968), amount of smiling and nodding one's head (Rosenfeld, 1967), moving hands, eyes, etc. (Condon & Ogston, 1966; 1967) and similarity in posture (LaFrance & Broadbent, 1976). Furthermore, there is a tendency to match up the content or types of conversation. Bales (1950) found that jokes lead to jokes, laughing leads to laughing, opinions lead to other opinions, and so on. Thus there is a goodly amount of matching of all kinds in conversations, and such matching facilitates the interaction and reduces the ambiguity concerning what is to be said or done next. The results regarding the content of conversations are also consistent with the findings of Bakeman and Dabbs (1976) regarding the type (looking, talking, etc.) of behavioral sequences.

There are a number of movements that occur in conversation that accompany the verbal material and clarify or emphasize its content. Baton-type movements of the hand (sometimes using the whole arm, other times using the hand only, depending on the person's culture) are used to emphasize points and accompany the rhythm of the speech (Efron, 1972; Scheflen, 1964). There are also concomitant raising and lowering of the head and eyelids to reflect questions and yielding of the floor.

In one study of conversations it was found that short verbal responses ("I see," "uh-huh") tended to come almost always at the end of a grouping or cluster of words (Dittman & Llewellyn, 1968). These words were almost always accompanied by head nods in an interesting way—listener head nods preceded listener verbalization. Dittmann and Llewellyn speculated that the head nods were a manifestation of the listener's readiness to respond. However, at the same time the listener was reluctant to talk until the speaker had finished. The nod acted as an interim acknowledgement that the message was understood.

Figure 7. A model of conversation based on the assumption that each person's response (R) is influenced by both what the person said before and how the other person responded to it.

Thus the conversation goes back and forth, each utterance by person *A* acting as a stimulus for the response by person *B* that follows, which, in turn, is a stimulus for person *A*. This sequence can be depicted as follows: $A \rightarrow B \rightarrow A \rightarrow B \rightarrow A$ and so on. However, what *A* said last time will effect *A* as well as *B*, if for no other reason than that people in this culture frown on people repeating themselves. Thus we have each statement being a response both to what the other person has just said and done and to what the speaker said earlier (see Figure 7).

Furthermore, there is also the intention and general goal of what each person would like to have come out of the conversation. That concern is in addition to the individual's response to his or her own and the other person's earlier statements and behavior (see Figure 8).

Thus a person's behavior in an ongoing conversation is affected by three sources: (1) his or her general goals and expectations, (2) the person's response to what he or she has already said earlier and what remains to be said, and (3) the responses of the other person. It takes skill to maintain some balance between these various components. The person who attends too much to his or her own goals and previous pronouncements gives the other person the feeling of being lectured to or manipulated. The bore could also be categorized as one

Figure 8. A model of conversation based on the assumption that each person's response (R) is influenced by (a) the person's goal for the conversation, (b) what the person said before, and (c) how the other person responded to it.

who is too concerned with personal goals and not concerned enough with the ideas of the other person. At the other extreme, too much of a person's responses being affected only by the other person's responses can lead to both losing track of the direction of the conversation, for example, "Now, how did we get on that topic?"

The kind of model of conversation depicted above is rudimentary and leaves out many other factors, but it has utility in describing and analyzing conversations. Attempts have been made to write computer programs that can simulate a person interacting with another. The program is written to follow a certain kind of therapeutic style, such as nondirective or reflective therapy. At the beginning it types out a message, such as:

> "Hello, I am your therapist. What seems to be the problem?"
> "Well, my girl friend and I haven't been getting along very well lately."
> "How long have you and your girl friend been having difficulty getting along?"
> "Well, it has been happening on and off for the last three months, but it really came to a head last week."
> "How do you feel about the fact that you and your girlfriend have been having difficulty getting along?"

TERMINATION

Most interactions terminate almost before they begin, that is, they consist of little more than the stroke exchanges described by Berne (1964, p. 37):

> "Hi!"
> "Hi!"
> "Warm enough forya?"
> "Sure is. Looks like rain, though."
> "Well, take cara yourself."
> "I'll be seeing you."

Most encounters are short-lived, and even those that go beyond the two- or three-stroke encounter described by Berne usually last less than a minute. At some point in the interaction, one person becomes aware of a need to leave or terminate the meeting. What is done to facilitate such an occurrence? How can the conversation be terminated gracefully?

There is little research on leave-taking, but one study does address that problem directly (Knapp, Hart, Friedrich, & Shulman, 1973). These researchers had subjects interview either equal- or higher-status confederates and were told that the amount of money they were paid depended on the accuracy and speed of their "attitudinal readings" of the interviewee. The interviewer had to get the information and get out as soon as possible. The confederate interviewee was instructed to give out no terminating or leave-taking cues during the interview no matter what the interviewer did.

Both the verbal and nonverbal behavior of the interviewer were coded and analyzed. The 45 seconds before the interviewer stood up to leave were divided into three 15-second segments. The time it took to leave after standing up represented a fourth time period for analysis. The first question was "What kinds of behavior increase as the person gets ready to get up to leave?" They found that the most common things the person does just before rising are break eye contact and lean forward. There was also a dramatic increase in major leg movements. Following standing up, individuals engaged in somewhat different behaviors as they tried to get themselves out of the room gracefully. His body orientation turned more toward the door, they broke eye contact often, smiled, and shook hands.

Hitting one's knees with both hands or the floor with one's feet (called "explosive hand contact" and "explosive foot movements") with or without a hearty "Well!" did not occur as often as expected. "Leveraging" (placing hands on knees, legs, or chair in such a way that they could be used to assist in standing up) was also relatively uncommon, but it did show a noticeable increase just before the person stood.

Although they are not our focus of attention, there were some interesting findings regarding verbal responses as the interviewer tried to terminate the interview. Reinforcement ("yeah," "right," "uh-huh," "sure," "OK") was the most common verbal category used during the final minute of exchange.

The most common sequence for terminating consisted of a reinforcement ("Yeah"), followed by a buffing term ("well"), which, if the relationship was a formal one, was followed by appreciation ("I really want to thank you") or an internal legitimizer ("I guess I'm finished"), or an external legitimizer ("I can see you're busy, so I'll leave"). If the relationship was an informal one, the interviewee followed the buffing ("well") with a welfare-concern statement ("take it easy") and/or continuance ("I'll see ya later").

Well, it appears that we have discussed the major ways in which nonverbal behavior functions to regulate social relations. *So,* we will now move to a consideration of the relationship between emotions and nonverbal behavior.

CHAPTER 5

Emotions and Nonverbal Behavior

The attempt to understand emotions is not a new concern for psychology. Although centuries of philosophical speculation preceded him, William James's (1908/1950) theory of emotions provides a starting point for a discussion of the psychology of emotional behavior. That theory stimulated considerable theoretical controversy and helped to initiate a whole area of research on emotions. One probable reason for the substantial interest in James's theory is that it is counterintuitive, that is, the theory's description of the development of emotional experience runs counter to common sense. In particular, James proposed that we feel an emotion because our bodily responses involve a particular pattern of activity which informs us of what we are feeling. That is, we are sad because we cry or we are happy because we are laughing and smiling, and not the opposite. The bodily changes which James believed to be critical to the feeling of an emotion included both overt motor activity, such as smiling, clenching a fist, or running, and internal physiological reactions involving changes in heart rate or visceral activity. The patterns of neural feedback from these bodily changes were believed to be specific enough so that different patterns identified different emotional states.

James's theory was the subject of an important critical evaluation by Cannon (1927). Cannon suggested several problems with James's position, including the following: (1) the viscera are not sufficiently sensitive to transmit the discriminating feedback necessary for identifying a particular emotion; (2) the same types of visceral changes seem to be present in very different emotional states; (3) even when the viscera can be separated from the central nervous system, emotional experience may still remain intact; (4) when the viscera are stimulated by artificial means, emotional states do not necessarily result; and (5) emotional experience seems to occur more quickly than the changes in the viscera. The first two problems—the insensitivity of the viscera and the similarity of visceral changes across different emotions—directly conflict with the basic assumptions of James's theory of emotions. While Cannon supplemented his criticism of James with a theory of his own, Cannon's theory of emotion has received relatively little attention. It is basically a neurophysiological approach to emotion and, as such, does not deal with the psychological aspect. Mandler (1975, pp. 100–101), in discussing James's and Cannon's positions, noted that both men contributed to a better understanding of emotional behavior. James helped to identify the role of autonomic arousal in emotionality, while Cannon clearly refuted the view that emotions could be identified with the perception of visceral arousal.

While James's theory was shown to be inadequate, Cannon's neurophysiologically oriented theory could not fill the gap as a comprehensive psychological theory of emotion. It was Schachter (1964) who provided a new approach to emotional behavior by integrating the cognitive aspects of feeling to the physiological changes experienced by the individual. Basically, Schachter proposed that physiological arousal was a necessary component in the experiencing of an emotion, but the arousal, by itself, could not define a specific or feeling state. It was the individual's cognitions about the social setting in which arousal occurred that permitted the arousal to be labeled in some specific manner. Thus, according to Schachter, the experiencing of an emotion was much more than the internal neurophysiological changes which occur when an individual is aroused.

An ingenious experiment by Schachter and Singer (1962) illustrated how the arousal and cognitive components interact to produce feeling states. Arousal was manipulated through the injection of either a placebo or epinephrine, a substance initiating autonomic activity. In addition, the subjects were given different expectancies for the causes of arousal and placed in different situations to facilitate specific cognitions for labeling the arousal. Basically, Schachter and Singer found that subjects, either uninformed or misinformed of the basis for their arousal, showed behaviors and reported moods indicative of either anger or euphoria, depending on the social context. That is, subjects experiencing arousal but having no convenient interpretation for it labeled it as euphoria when the situational cues (the behavior of a confederate) suggested euphoria and anger when different confederate cues indicated anger. In contrast, subjects who received correct information about what to expect following the injection showed both less emotional behavior and smaller mood changes than the subjects not correctly informed about the injection. Apparently the correctly informed subjects, though physiologically aroused, had an adequate explanation for their state and did not have to label it in terms of the setting.

Schachter's cognition-arousal theory of emotions was a distinct advance in understanding the process of emotional behavior, but some important questions still remained. For example, it seems clear that the role of cognitive activity in the process of emotional experience is not limited to merely evaluating or labeling the arousal. Cognitions about the stimuli or events producing arousal can have a substantial effect on the degree of initial arousal experienced (Leventhal, 1974; Mandler, 1975). This was illustrated in a study examining reactions of subjects to a stressful film showing a primitive initiation rite (Lazarus & Alfert, 1964). Both physiological arousal, as measured by heart and skin conductance, and negativity of mood ratings decreased when a commentary denying the harshness of the initiation rite was added to the otherwise silent film. The decrease in both the arousal and negative affect of the subjects was even greater when the film was preceded by the denial commentary. Thus the level of arousal produced was clearly limited by the types of cognitions individuals had about the film.

While Schachter directed attention toward the cognitive side of emotions, others, particularly Valins (1966, 1967a,b), carried Schachter's position a step further and suggested that the appropriate cognitions alone, without arousal, may be sufficient to experience emotion. Specifically, Valins (1966) proposed that actual autonomic arousal was not necessary to experience an emotion, as long as individuals *thought* they were aroused. In that study, Valins used false feedback of cardiac rate changes to influence male subjects' judgments of the attractiveness of slides of seminude females. On selected slides, subjects heard noticeable heart rate changes which were previously programmed by the experimenter. When the subjects were asked to select the most attractive females, there was a clear preference for those slides on which heart rate increases were heard. Valins interpreted this attribution of attractiveness as an indicator of affective experience and concluded that an emotional reaction could be precipitated by the appropriate cognitions, that is, belief in arousal change, independent of actual arousal change.

A procedural problem with the Valins study suggested by other researchers was that the attribution differences may have been mediated by actual changes in arousal, facilitated by the false feedback (Goldstein, Fink, & Mettee, 1972). However, an even more important problem with Valins's position may be a lack of conceptual clarity in distinguishing attribution from emotional experience. Harris and Katkin (1975) proposed that autonomic arousal was a necessary component for experiencing an emotional state, or what they termed "primary emotion." In contrast "secondary emotion" does not necessarily involve physiological arousal but may be cued by situational stimuli or by false physiological feedback, as in the Valins study. While primary emotion necessarily involves an individual's recognition and appraisal of arousal, secondary emotion may be manifested by only some components of arousal, such as attributions or self-reports, without any accompanying physiological arousal (Harris & Katkin, 1975). Thus, according to this distinction between primary and secondary emotion, what we commonly experience as an emotional reaction, for example, joy, sadness, or embarrassment, involves a necessary arousal component. However, reactions often correlated with those emotional experiences, such as attributions regarding various stimulus events, may occur without any necessary arousal.

The development of theoretical conceptions of emotional behavior over the last 15 or 20 years has clearly emphasized the role of cognitive determinants of emotions. However, it seems likely that arousal changes are a necessary link in the experiencing of an emotion. A final concern, which will have relevance for our later discussion of nonverbal behavior, is the issue of identifying the functional stimulus producing arousal change. In this discussion, we will rely heavily on Mandler's insightful treatment of the process of emotional behavior.

In general, Mandler (1975, chapter 4) proposes that any perceived stimulus input automatically initiates a "meaning analysis," or evaluation. However, the stimulus inputs which are particularly critical for the individual are those which interrupt some ongoing behavior or the plans for some behavior. It is the disruptive effect of the interruptive stimuli which precipitates arousal. Thus, Mandler proposed that the interruptive quality of a stimulus is common to all events initiating arousal, whether they are ultimately experienced as positive or negative states. Of course, the final experience flowing from the arousal change is a product of the cognitions surrounding the precipitating events. The usual meaning analysis following any stimulus input is necessarily more extensive when the input is an arousal-producing interruptive event because interruptions are of greater importance to the individual than noninterruptions; by definition, interruptions disturb the completion of behavioral sequences or plans for behavior.

This extensive meaning analysis, which evaluates the interruptive event and its subsequent arousal, can be seen as equivalent to Schachter and Singer's (1962) labeling process. Mandler's (1975, chapter 8) description of the experience of anxiety is a particularly informative illustration. Like other emotional experiences, anxiety begins with some interruptive input which produces arousal. However, specific to anxiety is the inability to "solve" the interruption in terms of substituting other behaviors or plans to permit the completion of some organized sequence of behavior. In other words, the individual lacks control and organization in a situation. It is this basic disorganization or helplessness which Mandler believes constitutes the experience of anxiety.

While this discussion of emotions is far from comprehensive, it should give the reader some flavor of the changing views of emotion and a sample of some of the current problems in researching emotion. As might be expected, with the relatively recent emphasis of cognition on emotional experience has come a considerable interest in social psychological factors affecting emotions. Consequently, much recent research is focused on variables such as the influence of the behavior of others, situational factors, and informational or instructional manipulations on the evaluation of arousal changes.

NONVERBAL INDICATORS OF EMOTIONALITY

This next section will review those nonverbal behaviors which seem to be reliable indicators of various emotional states. The various categories of behavior which permit us to "read" the emotional reactions of others include facial expressions, gazing behavior, body movement, paralinguistic behavior, and interpersonal distance. It should be noted that the relationship between various nonverbal behaviors and one affective reaction in particular, that of liking or love, was discussed in chapter 2.

Facial Expressions

The human face possesses a remarkable plasticity of expression. Subtle changes in the wrinkling of skin, tightening of muscles, movement of the mouth, or raising of the eyebrows can appear in an instant and vanish just as quickly. While we are all aware of this variety in facial expression, it is quite another issue to reliably interpret or decode such expressions. A number of studies using techniques such as live, videotaped, or photographic presentation of natural or role-played emotions have generally indicated considerable accuracy in judging emotional states from facial expressions. Ekman and his associates have generally found that observers could accurately determine whether photographed facial expressions came from pleasant or unpleasant situations (Ekman, 1965; Ekman & Bressler, 1972; Ekman & Rose, 1972). However, much more specific judgments of emotional state can also be made accurately. In fact, there is considerable information indicating that across a variety of cultures people can both accurately identify emotions from facial expressions and facially portray the emotions described by the experimenter (Ekman, 1972; Ekman & Friesen, 1971; Izard, 1971). The typical sample of emotions examined in these studies included happiness, sadness, anger, disgust, and surprise. Ekman (1975) states that while this evidence supports Darwin's (1872) claim of universality in facial expression, there are two ways in which facial expressions differ across culture. Specifically, both the situations eliciting various emotional states and the conventions prescribing the control or management of emotional expression can differ considerably across cultures.

For example, when Jacqueline Kennedy was seen as impassive and unemotional on television coverage of the funeral of John F. Kennedy, there was less criticism of her by American women than by women from other cultures. Being composed or reserved is a response to death that is within the range of acceptable behavior in the United States culture, even if it is not preferred by many Americans. But even though many Americans admired what they saw as courageous stoicism by Mrs. Kennedy, people from more emotionally expressive cultures interpreted her behavior as callous and unfeeling.

An experiment by Boucher and Ekman (1975) showed that different parts of the face may be critical to identifying differing emotional states. For example, viewing the brow and forehead alone were sufficient for accurately identifying surprise, while viewing the cheeks and mouth were sufficient for identifying disgust and happiness. The area around the eyes was critical for identifying fear and sadness, but no single area permitted an accurate identification of anger. Finally there is some research indicating that—at least in our society—females may be more accurate senders and receivers of emotion through facial expressions than males (Buck, Miller, & Caul, 1974; Buck, Savin, Miller, & Caul, 1972; Zuckerman, Lipets, Koivumaki, & Rosenthal, 1975). In other words, females seem to be more emotionally expressive and receptive than males, although the evidence is not overwhelming in that direction. It is possible that sex differences in developmental trends may permit emotional responsiveness in females but discourage it in males.

Gazing Behavior

Although the eyes are an important component of facial expression, it also makes sense to examine visual behavior in terms of eye contact initiated toward others in social interaction. In general, it seems likely that increased eye contact with others is indicative of more positive affective involvement (Argyle & Dean, 1965; Mehrabian, 1969). However, it may be difficult to convince new recruits in basic training that the hard stare of the drill instructor is a sign of benevolent concern. In such cases it is likely that the accompanying facial expression and the situational circumstances leave little doubt about the underlying disposition. The avoidance of eye contact in an interaction has been linked to a variety of emotional reactions, including embarrassment (Exline, Gray, & Schuette, 1965; Modigliani, 1971); disapproval (Pellegrini, Hicks, & Gordon, 1970); sorrow (Fromme & Schmidt, 1972); and anxiety or tension (Argyle & Dean, 1965; Fugita, 1974; Kleck & Nuessle, 1968). It is possible that when some of these negative emotional reactions are experienced, the avoidance of eye contact serves to minimize the individual's discomfort in the situation. The relationship of emotionality to another aspect of visual behavior, pupillary response, has been the object of considerable research. Hess (1965) has proposed that pupillary dilation is related to positive affect, while constriction is related to negative affect. Janisse (1973) has reviewed much of this research, including a number of studies showing results in opposition to Hess's hypothesis. Janisse concluded that increased dilation does seem to be related to affect, both positive and negative.

Body Movement

Relatively little research has focused upon the relationship between body movement and emotional state, but there is emerging evidence that some body movements may be related to negative affect. Kleck (1970) observed more self-manipulative behaviors (e.g., hand rubbing or scratching) in subjects interacting at closer distances to an interviewer and attributed that pattern to increased anxiety. In another study, object-focused hand movements (e.g., pointing away from the body) increased with increases in overt verbal hostility, while body-focused movements (e.g., rubbing the hands together) increased with increases in covert verbal hostility (Freedman, Blass, Rifkin, & Quitkin, 1973). Dittman and Llewellyn (1969) found that more head, hand, or foot movements occurred at the start of spoken clauses or in interruptions in them than during the actual flow of speech. Dittman and Llewellyn proposed that such movements may occur not only when there is difficulty in verbally encoding some complex idea, but also when there is pressure owing to various interpersonal concerns, such as creating a good impression. Those authors further suggest that body movements may generally indicate a spillover of tension in the situation. This proposal would fit well not only with the other results discussed in this section but also with our commonsense judgment that fidgeting is probably a reliable indication of discomfort.

Paralinguistic Behaviors

Considerable research has focused on the relationship of emotional states, particularly anxiety, to various content-free aspects of speech, such as errors, speech rate, and pauses. In terms of types of speech errors, Mahl's (1956) classification system has been widely used. A distinction has generally been made between Mahl's "ah" errors (occurrence of the sound "ah") and "non-ah" errors. The latter include sentence corrections, sentence incompletions, repetitions, stuttering, intruding incoherent sounds, slips of the tongue, and omissions. Several studies have shown that non-ah speech disturbances increase with increased anxiety (Cook, 1969; Feldstein & Jaffe, 1962; Kasl & Mahl, 1965; Siegman & Pope, 1965). In two studies, the incidence of ah disturbances—often referred to as "filled pauses"—was found to increase with increased anxiety. But results reported by Lalljee and Cook (1973) suggest a different interpretation: at least in the early stages of a verbal interaction, filled pauses may reflect linguistic uncertainty, which decreases over time in a given exchange. Of course it is possible that at different times the occurrence of filled pauses can reflect both the speaker's anxiety and his or her uncertainty in linguistic decision making. In addition, the use of ritualized units of speech such as "I mean," "really," and "well" may be linked to increased anxiety (Lalljee & Cook, 1973). In reviewing the relationships among talk, silence, and anxiety, Murray (1971) proposed a curvilinear relationship as the best fit between situational anxiety and verbal productivity. That is, verbal productivity seems to increase as anxiety arises, up to some moderate level, and then decreases for higher levels of anxiety. Finally, Davitz (1964) concluded, in his review of the vocal expression of emotions, that emotional meanings can be fairly accurately communicated by the vocal cues in speech, independent of the content. Techniques used in such research usually involve instructing a sender to communicate various specific emotions by repeating the alphabet or some constant nonemotional message, or distorting or masking the content of speech electronically while leaving the expressive characteristics intact.

Interpersonal Distance

As discussed in the chapter on liking, the distance between interacting individuals seems to be an important indicator of interpersonal attraction. However, additional evidence relating distance to other affective reactions is quite limited. In two separate studies, individuals who sat farther from an interviewer tended to rate themselves as more uncomfortable than those who sat closer (Patterson, 1973a; Patterson & Holmes, 1966). This relationship appears to directly oppose that reported by Kleck (1970), who found that subjects required to sit 4 feet from a confederate exhibited more behavioral signs of anxiety than did those seated at 10 feet. This inconsistency is really only apparent because individuals who are socially uncomfortable probably remain more distant from others, but enforced close proximity may precipitate discomfort, even among those normally at ease in social settings. In separate studies using role-playing procedures, fear enactment (Fromme & Schmidt, 1972) and approval avoidance (Rosenfeld, 1965) instructions increased the distance at which subjects interacted with a confederate.

Synthesis

Of course, in everyday interaction the critical issue is the manner in which the combined impact of all available cues works to facilitate the judgment of another person's emotional state. Both research findings and some common sense can help us to make some useful generalizations. First, the behaviors which will be most informative are those which are both variable in occurrence and accurately interpreted. Facial expression meets these two criteria better than any of the other behaviors discussed. Not only is there remarkable variability in facial expression, but also the differentiation of a number of facial expressions can be accomplished with a high degree of accuracy, as research by Ekman and his colleagues indicates. Vocal characteristics may also provide discriminating information, permitting the identification of several different emotional states. However, other cues, such as visual behavior, body movement, and some paralinguistic behaviors, while quite variable over time, are not usually sufficient by themselves for differentiating among a variety of emotional states.

That is, the presence or absence of one or more of these behaviors may indicate a change in emotional state, but a more accurate reading is probably dependent upon knowing the situational circumstances leading to the change and the previous behavior patterns of the individual involved. Interpersonal distance, compared to the other behaviors, is relatively invariant over time, particularly in seated interactions, and therefore is not generally a sensitive indicator of emotional changes.

While the communication of the specific type of affect may be most accurately accomplished through facial expression, the intensity of the affect seems to be communicated by body cues (Ekman, 1965). This suggestion is consistent with the earlier discussion of the limited informational utility of the behaviors other than facial expression. Furthermore, there is apparently a general awareness of the importance of facial expressions in trying to mask feelings or deceive others about our true feeling (Ekman & Friesen, 1974; Mehrabian, 1971). For example, excessive smiling may occur when one is trying to mask a feeling of anxiety (Mehrabian, 1971; Schulz & Barefoot, 1974). Although facial expressions can occasionally be effectively altered to deceive others, body movements, less subject to control than the face, can be used to read the deception (Ekman & Friesen, 1974). In conclusion, we can state that while facial expressions may be the most accurate indicators of feelings, they can also be easily changed to cover one's reactions. Other less differentiating cues, particularly body movements, provide information about the intensity of an emotional reaction, and because they are less susceptible to conscious monitoring, may signal attempted deception.

EMOTIONAL EXPERIENCE AND INTIMACY EXCHANGE

The discussion of the relationship of nonverbal behaviors to emotionality has, so far, been limited to focusing on those cues which signal various emotional states. In this section we will present an organized approach to the relationships among nonverbal behaviors, emotionality, and the process of intimacy exchange in social interaction. Specifically, the following discussion will examine the role of emotional reactions in mediating nonverbal exchange in interactions.

That is, in contrast to the earlier discussion of nonverbal indicators of emotional experience, this section will focus on the influence of emotional reactions on patterns of nonverbal exchange. This discussion will lead us to the analysis of a theory designed to explain and predict patterns of nonverbal exchange (Patterson, 1976). Before that theory can be presented and evaluated, we will have to trace some of the developments critical to its formulation.

Equilibrium Theory

One of the few attempts at a theoretical explanation of the relationships and functions of a variety of nonverbal behaviors was offered by Argyle and Dean (1965) in their equilibrium theory of intimacy. Argyle and Dean proposed that interpersonal intimacy or involvement is a cumulative product of a variety of behaviors, primarily nonverbal, including interpersonal distance, eye contact, leaning, smiling, and intimacy of conversational topic.

Equilibrium theory posits a kind of pressure between individuals for maintaining a comfortable level of interpersonal intimacy in the course of an interaction. This point of comfortable intimacy represents a balance between the approach and avoidance tendencies in the situation. Argyle and Dean suggested that approach forces may include the desire for visual feedback or the satisfaction of affiliative needs, while avoidance tendencies may include the fear of revealing oneself or of being rejected by others. Because intimacy is a composite of a number of specific behaviors, any one behavior can be altered to affect a change in total intimacy. However, once a comfortable level has been achieved, changes in any component behavior will require compensatory adjustments in some other behavior to maintain that comfortable level. The compensatory process can be likened to a hydraulic model, in which the total pressure, ideally, remains constant but can be differentially distributed. Of course, comfortable levels of intimacy will vary between different pairs of individuals and across different settings. However, independent of the levels involved, the broad general prediction from equilibrium theory is that, given a condition of disequilibrium in intimacy, directional compensatory adjustment will be made in one or more of the intimacy behaviors so that equilibrium can be restored.

Research on the equilibrium model of intimacy exchange has been generally supportive of its predictions (see Patterson, 1973b, for a review of the earlier studies). For example, situations in which subjects are approached closely or are the recipients of high levels of gaze usually produce compensatory adjustments. That is, in response to the initiation of increased intimacy by another person, subjects often turn away, decrease eye contact, or even leave the setting. However, a few studies have shown adjustments directly contrasting with those predicted by equilibrium theory (e.g., Breed, 1972; Chapman, 1975; Jourard & Freedman, 1970). In these instances, increased nonverbal intimacy produced not compensatory but rather reciprocal or enhancing responses. In other words, the increased intimacy by one member of a pair precipitated increased, not decreased, nonverbal intimacy in the other member. Although the exceptions to the general support for equilibrium theory are relatively few in number, they do present an important concern for the theory. It is clear that the nonverbal adjustments predicted by equilibrium theory occur often enough that the compensatory process cannot be rejected. At the same time, that process alone cannot explain the reciprocation or enhancement of increased nonverbal intimacy. What possible resolutions might be offered here? One factor which may be critical in explaining these contrasting adjustments to increased intimacy is arousal change and its subsequent role in emotional experience.

Nonverbal Intimacy and Arousal Change

An increasing amount of research on nonverbal intimacy has examined its effect on arousal. Whether the reactions are measured directly through monitoring physiological responses or indirectly through some behavioral or rating measure, there is a fair amount of evidence showing increased arousal resulting from increased intimacy. For example, closer approaches have been shown to increase electrodermal reactivity (McBride, King, & James, 1965); increased eye contact can similarly increase electrodermal reactivity (Nichols & Champness, 1971) and heart rate (Kleinke & Pohlen, 1971) and change EEG reactions (Gale, Lucas, Nissim, & Harpham, 1972). Behavioral and rating indicators of increased arousal in response to increased physical proximity have also been documented in several studies (Dabbs,

1971; Efran & Cheyne, 1974; Fisher & Byrne, 1975; Kleck, 1970). Although all these results show increased arousal resulting from increased intimacy, it seems likely that in at least some circumstances increased intimacy may precipitate decreased arousal. For example, holding or hugging one who is fearful or distressed probably decreases that person's arousal and improves his or her emotional state (Patterson, 1978a). For this reason, we will include the option for arousal decrease and consequently describe this process broadly as one of arousal *change*. At this point it may be appropriate to start putting the pieces of the theory together and evaluate its utility.

Arousal Model of Intimacy Exchange

The evidence just discussed, linking increased nonverbal intimacy to changes in arousal, provides the basis for the first assumption of this model. Specifically, sufficient changes in the intimacy behaviors of one person (A) precipitate arousal change in the other member (B) of a dyad. Arousal then becomes a necessary first step in mediating nonverbal adjustments to another's change in intimacy. Specifically, if B experiences no arousal change as a result of A's change in intimacy, the model predicts that B would not make any adjustments to A's change. If arousal change does result, it is assumed that the individual's cognitions about himself, the other person, or the situation channel that arousal change into a particular feeling state (Schachter & Singer, 1962). The type of emotion or feeling state experienced by B directs the course of adjustment made to A's change in intimacy.

From Figure 9 it can be seen that negative feeling states such as anxiety, discomfort, or embarrassment facilitate compensatory responses, that is, those predicted by equilibrium theory. In contrast, positive states such as liking, love, or relief facilitate adjustments characterized by the reciprocation or enhancement of the other's intimacy change. Of course, B's reactions, in turn, affect A and his or her subsequent response, as indicated by the feedback loop in Figure 9.

Two contrasting examples might serve to demonstrate the processes described in the theory. First, picture a situation in which you

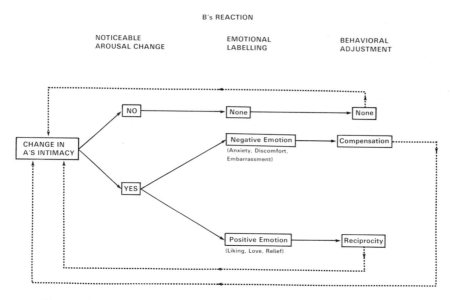

Figure 9. An arousal model of response to change in nonverbal immediacy.

are momentarily standing alone at a party when a stranger comes up, introduces himself and begins talking. This might normally be tolerable or even pleasant, but this person moves in very close, sustains a high level of gaze, and occasionally touches your hand as he is emphasizing some point. Most of us would feel uncomfortable in such a situation. Our attributions about this person might range from his being an obnoxious boor to the possibility that he is trying to make a pass (even in a same-sex encounter). Our theoretical model would assume that his increased intimacy initiated arousal change which was experienced as anxiety or perhaps just some vague discomfort. Short of leaving the setting it would be predicted that you could compensate for that intimacy by turning away or decreasing your gaze toward him. A structurally similar, but practically very different, incident might involve the same party setting, but instead of a stranger approaching you, it is now a good friend, lover, or spouse. The same behaviors described before now initiate a positively experienced arousal, for example, liking, which facilitates the reciprocation of increased intimacy. That is, you smile back, sustain a gaze toward the other person, and perhaps put your hand on his or her shoulder. Clearly, the two occurrences are experienced differently and responded to in contrasting fashions.

In summary, the arousal model of intimacy proposes that labeled arousal change mediates the type of behavioral adjustment resulting from another person's change in intimacy. Whether the behavioral adjustment is compensatory or reciprocal, it is assumed that both types of changes serve to maximize one's comfort or satisfaction in an interaction.

Critique of the Model

Although the arousal model has not been around long enough to permit an extensive amount of research on its predictions, a number of recent studies do provide some fairly good support for it. For example, friend-versus-stranger pairs of children viewing cartoons differed markedly in their interaction patterns. The friendship pairs matched (i.e., reciprocated) smiling, looking, and talking responses more than stranger pairs (Foot, Smith, & Chapman, 1977). These results were interpreted in terms of the positively valenced arousal (i.e., with friends) producing reciprocation of intimacy, while the less positively valenced arousal (i.e., with strangers) did not.

One study is particularly salient for the theory's focus on decreased as well as increased arousal-mediating patterns of nonverbal exchange. In that study, a postoperative recovery room in a hospital was used as the setting for manipulating a nurse's touch of the patient while the patient was (conveniently) being physiologically monitored. The results showed that male patients reacted to the nurse's touch with *increased* physiological arousal and more negative behavioral and judgmental responses, while female patients showed *decreased* physiological arousal and more positive related reactions (Whitcher & Fisher, 1979). Thus the differentially labeled *arousal change* was related to contrasting reactions, as predicted by the theory.

Although other research also provides evidence supporting the predictions of the arousal model of intimacy (e.g., Foot, Smith, & Chapman, 1977; Patterson, Jordan, Hogan, & Frerker, 1981; Storms & Thomas, 1977) there are some real limitations to the generalizability of the theory. First, it seems clear that expressing intimacy is but one of several functions of nonverbal behavior. That is, the same behaviors might be used in differing circumstances for other than expressing intimacy, and the theory would consequently not apply there. For example, touch might be used by a physician, chiropractor, or dentist in a professional-service capacity (Heslin, 1974), and the patient would not interpret it as intimacy-related. Alternately, increasing gaze toward someone or moving closer might simply be the most efficient ways of gaining more information about that person or what he or she is saying. In cases such as these, the arousal model may simply not apply.

Next, the relationship between the mediational components of arousal change and cognitive labeling is a problematic one. If some emotional reaction is, in fact, a necessary mediator, does the arousal change always have to precede the cognitive input, as Schachter and Singer (1962) propose? It seems unlikely that such a sequence always holds. As we discussed earlier in this chapter, cognitive input may precede and modify both the level of arousal and the negative affect experienced by subjects (Lazarus & Alfert, 1964).

Other unanswered issues concerning an evaluation of the arousal model of intimacy are discussed elsewhere (Patterson, 1978a). In summary, it is probably fair to say that this model offers some distinct advantages in terms of explanation and prediction, but revisions will almost certainly be required in our continuing attempts to understand intimacy exchange.

CONCLUSIONS

It is clear from the research discussed in this chapter that emotional reactions play an important role in the expression of different patterns of nonverbal behavior. Furthermore, this role seems to be a bidirectional one. That is, not only do people's nonverbal behaviors provide information about their feelings, but such behaviors can also trigger affective reactions in other people. In the former case, facial expressions and tone of voice can accurately inform us of another's emotional state. Other cues, such as gazing behavior, body movement, and some paralinguistic behaviors, probably enable us to broadly differentiate emotional from nonemotional reactions and may give us additional information about the intensity of any given emotional reaction.

The arousal model of interpersonal intimacy presents a framework in which to analyze the consequences of one person's nonverbal behavior. Basically this model proposes that sufficient changes in one person's intimacy behaviors relative to another person precipitate arousal in the latter person. That arousal, in turn, is experienced as either a positive or negative feeling state. Positive emotional reactions, such as liking, love, or relief should mediate a reciprocation of the other's change in intimacy, while negative emotional reactions such as anxiety or embarrassment should mediate compensatory adjustments. While this model is not designed to explain and predict all types of nonverbal exchange in social interaction, it does represent an integrated approach to some important aspects of nonverbal communication.

CHAPTER 6

Individual and Group Differences in Nonverbal Behavior

The purpose of the present chapter is to discuss some of the major factors affecting the role of nonverbal behaviors in social interaction. That is, while our intention in this volume is to try to discover and analyze the regularities in the social use of nonverbal behavior, we are all too aware of the limitations in generalizing these patterns across different circumstances. Another way of describing this concern is to appreciate that a number of factors interact with or moderate the patterns of nonverbal behavior discernible in various social processes. While the potential list of individual-difference variables could include a variety of different factors, this treatment will center on just three of them—culture, sex, and personality. Other factors such as age, socioeconomic status, or even occupation and religion may very well influence an individual's nonverbal expression, but culture, sex, and personality seem to be more important and consistent in their effect.

Before beginning a discussion of these group- and individual-difference variables, an important qualification should be mentioned regarding the interpretation of the influence of these factors on non-verbal behavior. Culture, sex, and personality are all subject variables, and as such are not easily manipulated in research. For example, sex-change operations have yet to catch on in the psychological laboratory. Invariably when one asks a question of how some subject variable is related to nonverbal behavior, individuals possessing different char-acteristics are deliberately *selected* for observation or testing. Thus we might try to choose individuals or groups from different cultures, males versus females, or subjects differing on one or more personality dimensions and examine potential differences in the way they behave. However, it is important to realize that even though we might find differences in terms of one of these dimenions, we cannot attribute the *cause* for those differences to that dimension. That is, individuals selected because of differences on one variable are also often different on a variety of other variables, and any one of these factors could be the more direct cause of specific behavioral contrasts. For example, take the case of cultural differences. Groups differing in cultural origin may also differ on general socioeconomic levels, educational opportunities, religion, climate, population density, and countless other factors.

If the pursuit of individual-difference variables does not enable the researcher to establish causal links to distinct patterns of nonverbal behaviors, then why even investigate such factors? One basic reason is that the description of relationships between subject variables and nonverbal behavior may provide important opportunities for a better understanding of individual differences. Systematic observation of nonverbal behavior, particularly in field settings, often provides an unobtrusive, nonreactive means of assessing individual differences. In such circumstances, the researcher's primary interest is in detecting and understanding individual differences, and observation of the nonverbal behaviors provides a means of doing that. However, as we mentioned earlier, our primary interest in reviewing culture, sex, and personality is to examine how these factors may differentially affect nonverbal social behavior. In this way, it may be possible to isolate and explain some of the inconsistencies apparent in the general patterns of nonverbal behavior.

CULTURE

Proxemics and Cross-Cultural Comparisons

Much of the current attention to the role of culture in nonverbal social behavior can be attributed to the insightful work of E. T. Hall (1963, 1966, 1968). Hall (1963) is credited with coining the term *proxemics* to encompass the study of human structuring of space. While

Hall seems to focus primarily on space, he clearly emphasizes the relationships between spatial behavior and other nonverbal behaviors. For Hall, spatial arrangements in social interaction are significant not so much for themselves but for the limits such arrangements set on a variety of different sensory functions. That is, space becomes the medium for controlling a variety of sensory components in interaction. In general, as one moves from the closer interaction distances to the farther ones, the potential for intimacy or immediacy with others decreases in all sensory modes. The four zones—intimate, personal, social-consultive, and public—are differentially used depending on factors such as the setting, activity, and the relationship between interactants. However, Hall's primary interest in analyzing and describing these interaction zones was to apply the system to cultural differences and attempt to understand the basis for such differences.

Hall's own observation of interactions in a number of countries suggested a basic dichotomy in the manner in which different cultures use space. On the intimate or "contact" end of the scale are included Arabic, southern Mediterranean, and Latin American societies. The English and northern Europeans represent the less intimate or "noncontact" societies. Americans apparently fall somewhere between the two extremes, but closer to the noncontact end. Hall's description of Arab interactions is not only informative but quite astounding to the average American or European who has had no exposure to that society. Typical Arab interactions are highly intimate, involving face-to-face orientations at a distance close enough to feel the breath of the other person (Hall, 1966, chapter 12). Touching, animated gestures, and loud voices are also common. By contrast, people from the noncontact cultures seem very aloof, cold, and literally distant. The actual difference in interaction distances between the two extremes may be several feet.

Although Hall's reports and descriptions of cultural differences in the use of space and other nonverbal behaviors are personal and anecdotal in nature, there are empirical studies addressing the same issue. For example, in a study comparing patterns of interaction between Arab and American male students, the Arabs were observed to sit closer to one another, maintain more direct body orientations, engage in greater eye contact, and converse in louder voices than did their American counterparts (Watson & Graves, 1966). Furthermore, the Arab pairs occasionally touched one another (perhaps accidentally), but even accidental touching was never present in the American pairs.

Additional support for Hall's hypothesized contact–noncontact distinction can be found in two different studies. In the first one, Cook (1970) replicated a questionnaire study on seating arrangements by Sommer (1965) and compared his English subjects with Sommer's American subjects. When the hypothetical interaction involved either a cooperative or conversational activity, Sommer's American subjects chose positions which were more intimate than Cook's English subjects. The second study, consisting of a figure-placement task, compared Greek and Italian students, as representatives of contact cultures, to Scottish and Swedish students, as representatives of noncontact cultures. Consistent with Hall's impressions, the Greek and Italian subjects placed the figures closer together than the Swedish and Scottish subjects did (Little, 1968). Finally, in another study of live interactions, the prediction of closer interactions between Latin American students than between North American students was not supported (Forston & Larson, 1968). However, the experimenters observed that, outside of the structured interaction sessions, the Latin Americans appeared to interact at closer distances than the North Americans did.

Subcultural and Ethnic Comparisons

It is tempting to extrapolate beyond the relatively distinct cross-cultural comparisons to potential subcultural differences in a racially and ethnically diverse society such as the United States. In fact, Hall (1966, chapter 13) has suggested that Puerto Ricans and Blacks are typically more involved or intimate with one another in interaction than are white Americans of northern European heritage. However, the results of several investigations comparing ethnic groups in the United States are equivocal with regard to this prediction. Without getting into all of the complicated details of these studies, there is conflicting evidence suggesting both closer interactions among Blacks than whites (Aiello & Jones, 1971; Bauer, 1973; Jones & Aiello, 1973; Smith, Willis, & Gier, 1980) and either the opposite or no differences at all (Baxter, 1970; Jones, 1971; Willis, 1966). While the contrasting results certainly prevent any clear conclusions about the possibility of ethnic or racial differences in the use of space, there are at least some clues suggesting possible bases for these inconsistencies. For example, Scherer (1974) found no differences in spatial behavior of Black and white school children when the socioeconomic status of the subjects was controlled. Furthermore, these studies also differed in the age and sex compositions of the various groups compared. Thus, it seems clear that potential differences related to subcultural or ethnic identity must be separated from other possible influences such as socioeconomic status, sex, and age of the interactants. A final point should be made regarding subcultural and ethnic differences, although it may already be obvious. Racial or ethnic differences between groups within a given society cannot generally be expected to be as distinct as those between the same racial or ethnic groups in their indigenous societies. The fact that different ethnic groups, even if relatively isolated, share some common experiences within a given society is likely to produce greater similarity than if they shared no common experiences.

Evaluating Cultural Differences

The description of the research on cultural and subcultural influences seems to lead to a judgment that the cultural, but not subcultural or ethnic, differences are related to distinct patterns of nonverbal behavior. However, it is premature to leave this topic without asking two critical questions: (1) Why do such differences (if any) occur? (2) How widespread or generalizable are the differences reported by various researchers? The latter question is one directed at the external validity of these results.

The first question is a very important one, especially when dealing with such a comprehensive factor as culture. Just what is it that is different about various cultures which predisposes its members to use nonverbal behaviors so differently? Hall (1968) has proposed a very intriguing hypothesis to account for the cultural distinctiveness reported in patterns of nonverbal behavior. Specifically, Hall suggested that these differences are grounded in the selective emphasis of different sensory modalities in various cultures. Thus, the reason for the close and intimate interactions among people in contact cultures might be found in their greater reliance upon tactile and olfactory cues. Conversely, for those in the noncontact culture, visual information may be more critical, requiring a greater separation between interactants for the comfortable and full-view focusing of the other person. According to Hall's view of the dynamics for these cultural differences, the particular sensory modalities emphasized within a given society structure not only the patterns of interaction but also a variety of other experiences. Consequently, we should be able to find other manifestations of the preference for specific types of sensory information within a culture which are consistent with the patterns observed in interaction. Hall does provide some examples in painting, sculpture, and architecture which seem to fit an overall pattern consistent with the differences reported in nonverbal behavior. However, the selective use of such examples, while informative, does not provide a really adequate test of Hall's notions. Nevertheless, going beyond a description of differences to some explanation of the dynamic processes accounting for them is an important step in generating researchable hypotheses.

There are, undoubtedly, other reasons which might be proposed for explaining cultural differences in nonverbal behavior. More situationally specific mechanisms might be tied to differences in socialization which are manifested directly or indirectly in terms of the nonverbal components of social behavior. However, one would still want to determine the *reason* for such socialization differences and identify the specific role of nonverbal behaviors in the whole process. In discussing individual differences in nonverbal behaviors, whether it is with respect to culture or other factors, it is all too easy to remain at a level of describing differences, without trying to identify the underlying reasons for them. Whether or not Hall's hypothesis regarding cultural differences in proxemic behavior can be supported, such attempts are clearly needed in pursuing our understanding of nonverbal behavior.

The second issue of interest in evaluating the research on cultural differences focuses specifically on the generalizability of the patterns observed. In other words, are the behavior patterns which have been observed for any given culture truly representative of a broadly based cultural style? It is probably fair to say that there is just not enough evidence available to answer this question confidently, but there is at least some basis for being skeptical about the generalizability of the results reported up to this time. For example, most of Hall's observations seem to be based on male interactants from apparently middle- or upper-class backgrounds—students, businessmen, or artists. Even the one controlled laboratory study (Watson & Graves, 1966) supporting Hall's observations involved Arab males who were students in the United States—a sample similar in sex and background to those originally described by Hall. It seems very unlikely that Arab females, at least those brought up under the more traditional customs, would interact as intimately and intensely with others as do the Arab males whom Hall describes. The same sort of problem exists in trying to generalize from any relatively small, homogeneous sample to the entire population. This difficulty is not unique, of course, to the cultural comparisons under review here. Anyone reading contemporary psychological research of an experimental nature might wonder if the ubiquitous college sophomore represents a majority of our population. At any rate, some caution is appropriate in evaluating the generalizability of the cultural differences reported. It seems very likely that differences in the sex of the interactants, situation, and possibly social class may all moderate some of the apparently distinct patterns of nonverbal behavior documented as a function of culture.

SEX DIFFERENCES

The influence of the sex of interactants on patterns of nonverbal behavior seems to be relatively pervasive. It appears that differences in nonverbal behavior as a function of sex are the rule rather than the exception, but there are a variety of other determinants which qualify any simplistic conclusions on this issue. The majority of the research on sex differences relates to contrasts in one or more component behaviors observed in various types of social settings, that is, differences focused on the interactive use of nonverbal behaviors. However, there are also some interesting sex differences in the ability to encode and decode affective reactions to various stimuli. The discussion in this section will be divided between these two general issues.

Sex Differences in Interaction

Perhaps the easiest way to begin this discussion is to limit ourselves initially to an analysis of sex differences in same-sex pairs or groups. In general, females engage in higher levels of nonverbal intimacy with one another than males do. For example, in same-sex dyads females have been observed to interact more closely than males (Aiello & Aiello, 1974; Aiello & Jones, 1971; Dosey & Meisels, 1969; Pellegrini & Empey, 1970). In fact, interactions which occur at 8 to 10 feet or more appear to be sufficiently uncomfortable for females that they may withdraw by avoiding eye contact (Aiello, 1977). This difference in interaction distance has also been found for groups larger than dyads (Giesen & McClaren, 1976; Mehrabian & Diamond, 1971; Patterson & Schaeffer, 1977). Another manifestation of the higher levels of intimacy between females is the presence of greater eye contact than that among males (Exline, 1963; Exline, Gray, & Schuette, 1965; Libby, 1970). In addition, it appears that females touch and are touched by others more than males and respond more positively to touch than do men (Fisher, Rytting, & Heslin, 1976; Jourard, 1966; Whitcher & Fisher, 1979).

Consistent with this general preference for higher levels of intimacy among females than among males is the result that females respond more favorably than males to crowded conditions in small groups (Freedman, Levy, Buchanan, & Price, 1972; Ross, Layton, Erickson, & Schopler, 1973). However, there is some evidence that the relatively positive reaction of females to the high-density group settings may be limited to activities having a social focus rather than a task or problem orientation (Marshall & Heslin, 1975).

Before we begin to examine some of the more complex aspects of sex differences in nonverbal behavior, it may be useful to consider briefly some of the potential causes for the basic differences described up to this point. While it is not easy to rule out any biological basis for these sex differences, it seems clear that early socialization into traditional sex roles has a considerable influence on the expression of nonverbal intimacy. Traditional norms emphasize the importance of independence, strength, competitiveness, and an orientation to task accomplishment in young boys, while young girls are typically taught to be more dependent, expressive, affiliative, and warm (Leibman, 1970). In addition, males learn to be more controlled in their relationships with other males apparently, in part at least, to avoid the potential inference of homosexuality. In contrast, the stigma of homosexuality is much less threatening for females, who, consequently, do not have to be so reserved in their intimacy with other females. There is some information that the sex differences in nonverbal behavior described here become fairly stable by the time that children reach adolescence (Aiello & Aiello, 1974). At that period, young people are particularly prone to peer influence, and consequently sex-role norms manifested in nonverbal social behaviors may become especially salient.

Sex differences are also apparent in opposite-sex interactions, although the patterns are somewhat more complicated and qualified. No attempt will be made here to duplicate the considerable coverage of nonverbal behavior across mixed-sex pairs as a function of attraction (see chapter 2). Rather, this discussion will examine the contrasts that might be drawn between male and female behavior within the mixed-sex pair. In studies examining comfortable approach distances in cross-sex pairs, females have been found to approach less closely to males than to females (Dosey & Meisels, 1969), while allowing closer approaches to themselves than males do (Hartnett, Bailey, & Gibson, 1970; Mehrabian & Friar, 1969; Willis, 1966). Thus females seem to be more restrained than males, not only in actively approaching someone of the opposite sex but also in passively limiting the closer approach of such an individual. This pattern may be more representative of interactions between strangers or casual acquaintances of the opposite sex than of interactions between romantically involved persons. The difference just described seems consistent with the typical impression of traditional roles in cross-sex interactions. Specifically, males are usually seen as the initiators of behavioral sequences, while females traditionally assume the reactor's role. Even when the apparent involvement of the female in a mixed-sex interaction is greater than the male, for example, the common finding that females smile more than males, that is not necessarily an indication of the female initiating a change in intimacy (Weitz, 1976). In fact, Weitz suggests that the higher incidence of smiling in females may develop from feelings of anxiety, discomfort, and abasement. Because it is clear that smiling can be used to mask negative feeling states (Mehrabian, 1971; Schulz

& Barefoot, 1974), this relative difference in smiling may simply reflect less control and assurance on the part of females.

The more dominant and controlled pattern of males described here is, of course, not necessarily typical of all mixed-sex interactions. One of the potentially important qualifiers of this pattern is the sex-role attitudes of the interacting individuals. For example, LaFrance and Carmen (1980) found androgynous persons to show a blend of masculine (interrupting, filling pauses) and feminine (smiling, gazing) behaviors. Weitz (1976) has reported interesting results indicating the degree of perceived nonverbal warmth in interactions was related to the sex-role attitudes of the interactants. Men with liberal sex-role attitudes were judged as being nonverbally "warmer" in same- and opposite-sex interactions than men with conservative sex-role attitudes. The only significant effect in rating of females' nonverbal warmth was that women with more liberal sex-role attitudes were judged as "colder" with other women than were those who had more traditional sex-role attitudes. Weitz suggested that some women having liberal sex-role attitudes may feel less positive toward women, in general, to the extent that those other women are representative of the traditional role they have rejected. Additional results reported by Weitz (1976) indicate that even when females assume a more nonverbally dominant or warmer role in a cross-sex interaction, it may be an adjustment to the male partner's predisposition. In particular, ratings of female nonverbal dominance and warmth were negatively related to male personality scores on dominance and affiliation, respectively. Thus, women were more dominant with more submissive males and warmer with less affiliative males. The contrasting patterns of female submissiveness and lessened warmth held for the more dominant and affiliative males. This sort of adjustment pattern exercised by females as a function of the male's personality was not found for females with other females or for males interacting either with males or females.

Of course, the relative status, authority, or degree of expertise in some task or activity may all give some advantage to females in taking a more independent role in the expression of nonverbal dominance or warmth when interacting with males. The influence of the degree of relationship in mixed-sex pairs may also substantially affect the nonverbal patterns described in this section. This is an especially important consideration because the vast majority of data is based on interactions between strangers or casual acquaintances. One exception to this sampling is a questionnaire study on the perception of touching behavior in married students. A specific and rather surprising result of this study was that married men rated the reception of sexual touching as less pleasant than did married women (Nguyen, Heslin, & Nguyen, 1976). Essentially opposite results had been found in an earlier, similar study on single male and female students. This example emphasizes the importance of the degree of relationship on not only the patterns of nonverbal behavior but also on the affective reactions to those patterns.

Differences in the Encoding and Decoding of Affect

Whereas the general role of facial expression in the communication of affect was discussed in chapter 5, only passing mention was made of the apparent sex differences in the encoding and decoding of affect. Several studies report some evidence for females being more effective encoders and decoders of affective reactions via facial expression than are males. Let us take a closer look at this evidence and examine the potential underlying causes for these differences.

In a typical study investigating the communication of affect in facial expressions, a sender or encoder will view several different types of scenes (e.g., disgusting, beautiful, sad, horrible, tender, etc.) presented on slides or film. That individual's facial expressions are usually unobtrusively videotaped at the time of the presentation of the scenes and viewed, either simultaneously or later, by receivers or decoders. The task of the decoders is to classify the facial expressions into one of the categories of initiating stimuli. Although there are a number of studies showing females to be better decoders of emotional expression than males (see Hall, 1978, for a review of that research), the sex differences noted in encoding emotional expressions may be more theoretically interesting. Buck and his colleagues (Buck, 1975; Buck, Miller, & Caul, 1974; Buck, Savin, Miller, & Caul, 1972) and others using that paradigm (Fugita, Harper, & Wiens, 1980; Woolfolk, Abrams, Abrams, & Wilson, 1979), have found that at least in some circumstances females are more accurate encoders of spontaneous facial expressions than are males, that is, the facial expressions of females are more accurately identified than are those of males. However, other results show little advantage for female encoders (Thompson & Meltzer, 1964; Zuckerman, Hall, DeFrank, & Rosenthal, 1976).

It seems likely that a combination of factors may be responsible for the mixed results on encoding differences. First, one line of evidence suggests that those who are more accurate encoders show less physiological reactivity to the emotional stimuli than the less accurate encoders (Buck, Savin, Miller, & Caul, 1972; Notarius & Levenson, 1979). Because the majority of the low-reactive, high-accurate encoders (externalizers) in the Buck *et al.* (1972) study were females, while the high-reactive, low-accurate encoders (internalizers) were males, sex differences may be based on the link between physiological and expressive reactions. Consequently, Buck *et al.* (1972) suggested that males in our culture may be taught to be internalizers of affect, inhibiting or masking many emotions, while females have greater license to express outwardly their affective reactions. It is also possible that the active inhibition of outward expression by males may contribute to their higher internal or physiological reactivity. Some support for the social-learning basis for sex differences in expressiveness was indicated by Buck's (1977) finding of a negative correlation between age and encoder accuracy in boys age 4 to 6, but no relationship between age and encoder accuracy in girls of the same age range. That is, in the preschool years, young boys apparently learn to inhibit their expressiveness, while young girls continue to be relatively free in their expressiveness.

If males learn to be less expressive and in the course of doing so exhibit greater physiological responsiveness, then why aren't females uniformly better encoders of affect? The major qualification here may be the type of stimulus initiating the reaction, although its impact may be noted in two differing ways. First, some stimulus scenes, such as sexual slides presented to adults or unusual photographic or artistic slides, are probably more ambiguous or variable in their encoding. That is, the expressive reaction to such stimuli are more a product of individual differences in encoder experience and values than are a pleasant slide of a beautiful landscape or an unpleasant slide of an accident scene. Secondly, while it is assumed that females are generally more expressive than males, that pattern may be reversed for stimuli of a more hostile and aggressive nature (Buck, 1977). Thus the type of stimulus initiating the expressive reaction may limit or even reverse the typical advantage of females in encoder accuracy.

In summary, there is some evidence that females may be more accurate decoders and encoders of facial expression than males. The differences in encoding ability may also be related to differential physiological reactivity, with the better or more expressive encoders (typically females) being less physiologically responsive. Because the decreased internal reactivity may very well be a product of the increased overt expressiveness, and not vice versa, one has to be careful in interpreting this relationship. Finally, the relative advantage of females in encoding accuracy may be limited to stimuli which are not only unambiguous with regard to the pleasantness of their content but also fall within the appropriate sex-role constraints for the expression of affect.

PERSONALITY

It seems quite reasonable to consider personality differences as a potential source of influence on nonverbal behavior. No doubt many people have their own "theories of personality," which relate certain patterns of nonverbal behavior to distinct types of individuals. Impressions which focus on one person's "pushiness" or another's "shyness" typically have considerable meaning in terms of nonverbal behavior. Although there has been some general skepticism about the importance of personality *per se* in social behavior (e.g., Mischel, 1969), there has been a considerable amount of research focused on personality correlates of nonverbal behavior. Again, in reviewing this research, we have to be careful in making causal attributions linking different personality types to distinct patterns of nonverbal behavior.

Preliminary to discussing the specific relationships between personality characteristics and nonverbal behavior, it may be useful to examine the intraindividual stability of nonverbal behaviors. If patterns of nonverbal behavior can be related to specific personality characteristics, it would seem possible only to the extent that the relevant behaviors manifest temporal stability. In other words, we are likely to find relationships between personality and nonverbal behaviors only when there is consistency in the way people use nonverbal behaviors. Fortunately this does seem to be the case, at least for some behaviors on which we have such information. For example, in two separate studies focusing on the stability of approach distances in interview settings, the correlations between the first and second approaches were approximately $r = +.90$ and higher (Daniell & Lewis, 1972; Patterson, 1973a). The very high degree of stability manifested in these two studies covered intervals from 20 minutes to 2 weeks with the same interviewer. Even when different interviewers were employed, the stability coefficients still averaged approximately $r = +.80$ (Daniell & Lewis, 1972). Data on gazing behavior similarly indicates high levels of stability, both within a given interaction (Kendon & Cook, 1969; Libby, 1970) and across interactions (Daniell & Lewis, 1972; Patterson, 1973a). Finally, there is evidence that the degree of forward lean and body orientation in seated interactions are relatively stable over time (Patterson, 1973a). These findings on intraindividual stability over time essentially indicate that people apparently do use at least some of the nonverbal behaviors in a consistent manner. This does not mean, however, that situational influences such as the type of setting or activity cannot modify a common pattern of nonverbal expression.

Now that we have some information suggesting that people do use nonverbal behaviors consistently, we can go on to see if personality differences are predictive of different patterns of nonverbal behavior. First, we will examine how rather extreme and pervasive differences between groups of people might be related to different patterns of behavior. Included here would be comparisons between psychiatric and deviant groups versus normal groups. The remaining coverage will focus on more limited and specific comparisons within a normal range of personality differences.

Normal–Abnormal Differences

There is considerable evidence that psychiatric patients, particularly those diagnosed as schizophrenic and depressive, generally show less intimacy with others than do normal subjects. This typical pattern of avoidance is manifested by larger interpersonal distances

(Horowitz, Duff, & Stratton, 1964; Sommer, 1959), nonconfronting body orientations (Sommer, 1959) and lower levels of eye contact (Rutter & Stephenson, 1972; Waxer, 1974). There is an interesting issue relating to the dynamics behind these differences between normals and schizophrenic and depressive patients. Specifically, there is a question concerning whether the lower level of gaze initiated by such patients is part of a general pattern of avoidance of a wide range of stimuli or is specific to the avoidance of people? Williams (1974) tested these two explanations by observing gaze patterns in schizophrenic and control subjects in a waiting room. The control subjects were a mix of nonschizophrenic patients and a small number of hospital employees. The salient gaze targets were either a television program or the confederate. The proportions of television watching and occasional confederate-directed glances were comparable during the first part of the waiting period when the confederate was silent. However, once the confederate tried to initiate a conversation, substantial differences appeared in the gaze patterns of the schizophrenic and control subjects. While confederate-directed gaze increased in both groups, the increase for the controls was very noticeably greater. Conversely, the decrease in television watching in response to the confederate's comments was much less for the schizophrenic subjects. These findings are obviously consistent with the suggestion that the schizophrenic's gaze aversion is specific to other people and not indicative of a broader stimulus-avoidance pattern.

Interpersonal avoidance behaviors may also be typical of a very different kind of group—violent and aggressive individuals. In two separate studies, one with adult male prisoners and another with underachieving male adolescents, substantial differences in approach distances were found between the aggressive and nonaggressive subgroups (Kinzel, 1970; Newman & Pollack, 1973). The differences were particularly striking in the study with prisoners. In that study, the male experimenter sequentially approached each prisoner from eight different directions until the subject told him to stop. The average area, shown in Figure 10, required by the violent prisoners was over four times that required by the nonviolent prisoners. It is also clear these differences were not just the product of some casual judgment. Kinzel reported that several of the violent prisoners reported perceiving the experimenter "rushing" or "looming" at them as he

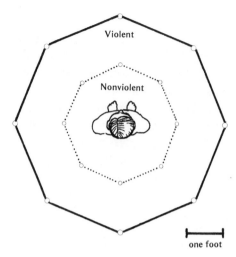

Figure 10. Body-buffer zones observed for violent and nonviolent prisoners. (A. F. Kinzel, 1970, Figure 3. Reprinted by permission.)

one foot

walked closer. Others clenched their fists, experienced goose pimples, or had to turn around to view the experimenter when he approached from behind. The violent group was also characterized by disproportionately larger rear-buffer zones. Kinzel interpreted the larger approach distances from behind as being a product of concern about homosexual attack, especially given this realistic fear in the prison context. However, anyone who is habitually violent may have a good reason in terms of general self-defense to fear others who approach from behind.

Personality Differences within Normals

The differences discussed up to this point represent rather pervasive contrasts between groups of individuals. As such, it is relatively difficult to identify one dimension, or even a few dimensions, which are specifically related to distinctive nonverbal patterns. In addition, it is obviously difficult to generalize the results to a more normal population. The remaining discussion of personality correlates of nonverbal behavior will focus on more limited personality differences within a normal range of individual differences.

At least one group of personality characteristics, including the dimensions of affiliation, introversion–extraversion, and social anxiety, seems to offer some hope for predicting nonverbal social behavior. Individuals scoring higher on affiliation scales apparently prefer closer seating arrangements than low scorers (Clore, 1969; Mehrabian & Diamond, 1971). In addition, there is also some evidence that high-affiliative females look more at others (Exline, 1963). The relationship between nonverbal intimacy and extraversion parallels that described for nonverbal intimacy and affiliation. Specifically, extraverts chose closer seating distances than introverts (Cook, 1970; Patterson & Holmes, 1966; Pedersen, 1973) and engaged in higher levels of eye contact (Kendon & Cook, 1969; Mobbs, 1968). In addition, increased levels of social anxiety have been marginally related to more distant approaches in an interview setting (Patterson, 1973b, 1977). While much of the evidence relating these three personality dimensions to nonverbal intimacy indicates only weak to moderate relationships, the convergence among these dimensions suggests a more common underlying pattern. That is, although affiliation, extraversion, and social anxiety are at least nominally distinct dimensions, a factor-analytic study showed that a majority of items from all three scales loaded on (correlated with) a common approach–avoidance factor (Patterson & Strauss, 1972). Consequently, these separate findings may reflect a shared pattern relating social approach–avoidance to nonverbal intimacy.

There are, of course, numerous other possibilities for examining personality correlates of nonverbal intimacy. For example, Friedman, Prince, Riggio, and DiMatteo (1980) have developed a 13-item test that is proposed to be a measure of expressiveness, outgoingness, nonverbal facility, and readiness to use nonverbal behavior. In general, much of the research on personality correlates has shown either relatively weak relationships to nonverbal behavior or relationships that, unfortunately, cannot be replicated. Another qualification in much of the personality research is the lack of a solid theoretical framework for interpreting the relationships that are found. There are two interesting exceptions to the general paucity of theorizing in this area which deserve to be covered in our discussion.

The first personality model is one offered by Duke and Nowicki (1972), which focuses specifically on the dimension of internal–external locus of control. Although Duke and Nowicki discuss this factor solely in terms of its relationship to interpersonal distance, it is probably legitimate to extend it to other nonverbal intimacy behaviors. The initial distinctions are based on Rotter's (1966) contrast between internals—those who perceive themselves as generally being in control of their own fate—and externals, who perceive themselves as generally being subject to forces outside of themselves. The basic assumption of the model is that the combined effect of internal–external control and situational expectancies influence the degree of preferred closeness to others. Specifically, internals and externals are predicted to act similarly in situations in which clear expectancies are present for the reactions of others, for example, interacting with friends or relatives. For settings in which specific expectancies are not available, however, for example, interacting with strangers, externals will be more reserved and distant than internals. This lessened intimacy for externals, compared to internals, in uncertain situations is apparently due to the lack of control they feel when interacting with strangers. Results from two studies reported by Duke and Nowicki (1972) supported these predicted differences in distancing by internals and externals. Related findings indicate that internal-control subjects were more likely to choose seats designated as leadership positions (Hiers & Heckel, 1977). In addition, internal-control subjects may be less affected by crowding than external-control subjects (Schopler & Walton, 1975). It will be interesting to see if further research not only supports the predicted differences in interpersonal distance but also extends the contrasts to behaviors such as eye contact, touch, smiling, and other cues.

A second approach is one that is based on the construct of self-monitoring (Snyder, 1974). Self-monitoring may be described as a dimension which reflects the tendency to manage one's behavior for beneficial self-presentation. The validity of Snyder's (1974) Self-Monitoring Scale has been examined and generally supported in a number of recent studies, but its application to nonverbal behavior is clearly demonstrated in a paper by Ickes and Barnes (1977). These researchers paired subjects on the basis of their self-monitoring scores and examined their interaction patterns during a staged waiting period. In general, the individuals who were higher in self-monitoring were likely to talk first, initiate later conversational sequences, feel more self-conscious about their behavior, and use their partner's behavior as a guide for their own actions. Females who were high in self-monitoring were more likely to be expressive with their gestures than were low self-monitoring females, but the opposite pattern seemed to hold for males. This effect suggests that the sex differences discussed earlier may be modified by a dimension such as self-monitoring. Thus both high self-monitoring males and females may be more attuned to their appropriate role behaviors and exhibit more dramatic sex differences than their low self-monitoring counterparts. While it is probably too soon to tell, the self-monitoring dimension could help us to identify individuals who are sensitive to a variety of interpersonal and situational cues and use those cues to regulate their own nonverbal expressiveness.

CONCLUSIONS

The individual–group difference dimensions of culture, sex, and personality represent potentially important qualifying factors which must be weighed in evaluating the generality of the various patterns of nonverbal behavior described elsewhere in this book. In many cases it is not simply the result of just one of these variables acting singly to influence some social process, but rather it is the combined effect of these and other factors which may produce an unusual or unexpected effect. For example, the effects of culture and sex on nonverbal behavior may interact to produce one kind of sex difference in one culture and little or no difference in another culture. This might be particularly the case where one is comparing a modern, technologically advanced society which tends to promote women's rights and opportunities to a more primitive, agricultural society which more severely limits the opportunities of women. Similarly, differences in personality *per se* may not be substantially correlated with changing patterns of nonverbal behavior. However, the interaction of personality and situation may be a very good predictor of nonverbal behavior. Thus, if one compares the levels of nonverbal intimacy demonstrated by internal- versus external-control individuals who interact with their good friends, few differences may be evident. However, in more potentially stressful or unpredictable situations, only the internals may continue to be relatively comfortable and expressive. In general, a sensitivity to these and other individual difference dimensions may help us to understand those all too frequent exceptions to the general patterns we have described.

CHAPTER 7

Theoretical Integrations and Practical Applications

In the previous chapters we examined the role of nonverbal behavior in various social psychological processes. Of necessity, these discussions have tended to be rather focused, and as a result, the commonalities across these various processes may not have been apparent to the reader. Nevertheless, it is possible to provide some theoretical integrations across our earlier divergent concerns. In developing this discussion it may be useful to review briefly several theoretical explanations before describing a new comprehensive approach to nonverbal behavior.

Two prominent theories—Argyle and Dean's (1965) equilibrium theory and Patterson's (1976) arousal model of interpersonal intimacy—were discussed in considerable detail in chapter 5. Common to both of them is a perspective which emphasizes the role of nonverbal behavior in contributing to interpersonal intimacy. The equilibrium model focuses specifically on the process of compensation which serves to maintain intimacy at some comfortable or appropriate level. That is, when one person's nonverbal intimacy is sufficiently divergent from the comfortable level, the other person will make compensatory behavioral adjustments designed to reestablish an equilibrium. The arousal model extends equilibrium theory by attempting to explain instances of reciprocity or matching of intimacy in addition to the compensatory changes. Specifically, the arousal model proposes that the particular form of adjustment to another's change in nonverbal intimacy is a consequence of the mediating influence of an arousal-attribution process. For example, a close approach by a stranger may precipitate arousal, which becomes negatively labeled as fear. That should result in a compensatory adjustment such as turning away or decreasing gaze. Conversely, a similarly close approach by a good friend or loved one would also precipitate arousal, but that arousal might be positively labeled as liking or love. Under these circumstances, the increased intimacy should be reciprocated by adjustments such as increased gaze, touch, or smiling.

Other more limited models also emphasize arousal and attribution processes. Specifically, Ellsworth and Langer (1976) have proposed that arousal and attribution mediate reactions to staring. In a similar fashion, Worchel and Teddlie (1976), in analyzing reactions to increased density, focus on the arousal and attribution mediators. They propose that crowding reactions are the product of personal-space violations, which precipitate increased arousal and an attributional analysis.

An alternate approach to describing the influence of interpersonal distance focuses on relational and situational variables (Sundstrom & Altman, 1976). Specifically, this model proposes that the degree of comfort felt to varying interpersonal distance is a function of the relationship between the interactants and their expectancy for interaction. In general, although friends are more comfortable at closer distances than are strangers, an inverted U curve describes the relationship between interpersonal distance and comfort for both groups. Further, among strangers not expecting to interact, increased comfort is directly related to increased interpersonal distance.

A most ambitious attempt at explaining patterns of nonverbal behavior is Cappella and Greene's (1980) discrepancy-arousal model of mutual influence. Cappella and Greene focus on a comprehensive group of nonverbal and verbal expressive behaviors. Their model is an elaboration of Stern's (1974) discrepancy-arousal theory, which was generated to explain infant–adult interactions. Central to this perspective is the assumption that arousal in interactions is a product of the discrepancy between the individual's expectations for the other person's behavior and the actual behavior of the other person. Little or no discrepancy should precipitate no arousal and consequently be perceived as affectively neutral. Moderate discrepancy is assumed to be moderately arousing and therefore pleasurable, while high discrepancy is assumed to be highly arousing and unpleasant.

In contrast to the arousal model of interpersonal intimacy, Cappella and Greene's model emphasizes the role of cognitions earlier in the mediational sequence, that is, the cognitive work is involved in evaluating the discrepancy. In this way, the amount of increased arousal *per se* determines the affective reaction of the individual, which, in turn, specifies the type of behavioral adjustment initiated. Specifically, little or no arousal is affectively neutral and requires no behavioral adjustment. Moderate arousal is experienced positively and precipitates reciprocation of the other's behavioral expressiveness, while the excessive and unpleasant arousal precipitates a compensatory adjustment in behavioral expressiveness. Although this model has yet to be tested, it does offer considerable promise for a more parsimonious explanation of contrasting patterns of nonverbal behavior.

It is not our intention here to try to evaluate the relative merits of these different models of nonverbal behavior. Instead, we have tried to describe briefly a range of models representing differing theoretical explanations. We will have to wait for the results of empirical studies to examine the accuracy and generalizability of specific predictions. However, substantive limitations in these various models are evident even now. For example, each of the models described here is limited in one or more of three specific characteristics: (1) the range of behaviors treated (e.g., gaze or distance); (2) the functions apparently underlying the patterns of nonverbal behavior; and (3) a specific consideration of predisposing factors influencing nonverbal exchange. With respect to the first point, the existing models typically focus only on one or, at best, a few of the many nonverbal behaviors which comprise the interactive process. Cappella and Greene's discrepancy-arousal model certainly fares better on this point. On the second issue, it appears that the models are either limited to one function (e.g., intimacy or crowding control), or a functional perspective is simply ignored. On the third point, all of the models are distinctly limited. Although Sundstrom and Altman (1976) specifically consider relational and situational factors, they do not integrate other potential predisposing factors into their model. There is commonly some appreciation of qualifying or limiting variables in these different models, but their exact roles are left indeterminate.

In an attempt to address some of the limitations of these theoretical models, one of us has recently developed a comprehensive approach to explaining patterns of nonverbal behavior in social interaction (Patterson, 1982). This theoretical framework may prove to be useful in analyzing nonverbal behavior in very divergent circumstances. For our immediate concerns in this book, this model may provide a general theoretical explanation of nonverbal exchange and suggest a useful means of classifying the issues discussed in the earlier chapters.

A MULTISTAGE FUNCTIONAL MODEL

A basic assumption underlying this model is that understanding a given interaction requires a focus broader than the immediate exchange between the participants. In particular, one must attend to what the individuals bring to the interaction in the form of their own personal characteristics and past experience. Furthermore, the constraints of the interaction setting and relationship between the interactants must be evaluated. Before we discuss how these influences relate to a functional approach toward nonverbal behavior, it may be useful to identify the behaviors focal to this theory.

A first step in developing a model for explaining the patterns of nonverbal behavior in interactions is defining the relevant range of behaviors. We have focused on a limited number of behaviors which seem most important in interaction. These behaviors, which we will term *nonverbal involvement behaviors,* include the following: (1) interpersonal distance, (2) gaze, (3) touch, (4) body orientation, (5) lean, (6) facial expressiveness, (7) talking duration, (8) interruptions, (9) postural openness, (10) relational gestures, (11) head nods, and (12) paralinguistic cues such as intonation, speech rate, volume, and so on. The first five behaviors coincide with Mehrabian's (1969) list of immediacy cues. Mehrabian defined immediacy as "the extent to which communication behaviors enhance closeness to and nonverbal involvement with another" (p. 203). Conceptually, nonverbal involvement is very similar to immediacy, but the involvement construct is clearly more comprehensive at the operational level. In general, increased involvement would be indicated by decreased distance, increased gaze, touch, more direct body orientation, more forward lean, greater facial expressiveness, longer speech duration, more frequent and/or more intense interruptions, increased postural openness, more relational gestures, more frequent head nods, and more intense paralinguistic cues. Of course, modifications will probably be made in this list, and the relative importance of the different cues probably varies across situations. With this behavioral construct defined, we can now move to a discussion of the heart of the model—functions served by nonverbal behavior.

Functional Classification

Analyzing nonverbal behavior in terms of its functions is certainly not a new approach. (For examples of earlier functional classifications see Argyle, 1972; Ekman & Friesen, 1969b; and Kendon, 1967.) The functional classification proposed here will necessarily overlap with some of the categories described by other researchers. However, some new distinctions will also be offered. The purpose of this classification is to provide a relatively comprehensive set of functions which can be related to the management of the involvement behaviors in social interaction. The specific functional categories proposed here are those of (1) providing information, (2) regulating interaction, (3) expressing intimacy, (4) exercising social control and (5) facilitating service or task goals. The last three, which might be described as molar functions, are most important in determining the purpose behind an interaction. We will discuss each of these in some detail and later describe their role in the multistage model.

Providing Information.   Perhaps the most basic function of nonverbal behavior is simply an informational one. From the perspective of the decoder or receiver of some nonverbal behavior, almost everything the actor or encoder does can be viewed as potentially informative. Many researchers make a distinction between *communicative* and *indicative* informational behavior. Although there is some general agreement on this distinction, the criteria used to define communication or indication differ considerably (Wiener, Devoe, Rubinow, & Geller, 1972). The distinction of particular utility for this functional

model is one which emphasizes either one of two related criteria—
purposive behavior (MacKay, 1972) or intention to communicate (Ekman & Friesen, 1969b). That is, if a behavioral pattern could be described as either purposive or intentional, it would be classified as
communicative. If not, it would probably *indicate* something about
the encoder, but the encoder could not be described as communicating
that information. For example, if a harried businessman wished to
"communicate" nonverbally that he wanted to terminate a particular
interaction, he might glance at his watch occasionally, fidget in his
chair, and check his appointment calendar. If the frequency or intensity of these cues increase up to the point when the visitor says he
has to leave and then abruptly stop, an observer might fairly confidently judge that those behaviors were purposive. That is, once they
had achieved their purpose, they were terminated. Such behavior,
meeting the criterion of being purposive, would be judged communicative. In contrast, if the same behaviors continued after the visitor
left, one could hardly claim that they were designed to make the
visitor leave. Instead, in the latter case, they would be described as
indicative; that is, those behaviors may indicate something about the
encoder (e.g., anxiety), but they should not be termed communicative.

Regulating Interaction.   The second function, and probably the
one that is most automatic and least reflective, is that of regulating
interaction. This term refers to the use of involvement behaviors in
both setting the behavioral structure of the interaction and influencing
momentary changes in conversation. In the former instance, behavioral structure or framework for interaction appears to be determined
substantially by its "standing features," which include distance, body
orientation, and posture (Argyle & Kendon, 1967). Although these
behaviors remain relatively stable over the course of an interaction,
they are important because they set some rough limits on the range
of involvement manifested through other nonverbal behaviors. For
example, greater distances in interaction make touch impossible, and
nonconfronting body orientations require somewhat greater effort to
sustain high levels of gaze. In contrast to the standing features, dynamic features such as gaze, facial expression, and verbal intimacy
affect the momentary changes in conversational sequences (Argyle

& Kendon, 1967). Many of these issues, reflecting the function of regulating interaction were discussed in chapter 4.

Expressing Intimacy. Much of the research on nonverbal behavior in interaction has developed from an intimacy perspective; that is, nonverbal involvement reflects the intimacy desired toward another. In general, intimacy might be described as a bipolar dimension reflecting the degree of union with or openness toward another person. Practically, increased intimacy is the result of greater liking or love for another, or greater interest in or commitment to such a person. Argyle and Dean's (1965) equilibrium theory and the arousal model (Patterson, 1976) focus on intimacy regulation and exchange. Generally, high intimacy is reflected in high levels of nonverbal involvement, but that is not always the case. Conversely, high nonverbal involvement may indicate something other than high intimacy. This latter circumstance will be considered in greater detail in discussing the next two functions. Representative of the typical link between intimacy and nonverbal involvement is Rubin's (1970) finding that couples who score higher on a romantic love scale (one aspect of intimacy) spent more time gazing into one another's eyes (nonverbal involvement) than those scoring lower. Similarly, in a review of spatial behavior, Patterson (1978a) reported that increased liking for or attraction to another person resulted in closer approaches, especially in female–female and male–female pairs.

Social Control. This function is one which has not been generally emphasized in previous discussions of nonverbal behavior. Social control may be described as the exercising of influence over other people. More specifically, this influence would be aimed at producing a direct reaction in trying to persuade others of one's viewpoint by, for example, implementing a moderately close approach, increased gaze, and appropriate paralinguistic emphasis to communicate a particular verbal message more effectively. Another example would be the use of gaze or touch to institute or reinforce status differences between individuals (Henley, 1973). A less direct means of producing a desired reaction in someone would be through the use of any one of a variety of self-presentation patterns designed to have others view an actor more favorably (Goffman, 1967, 1972). For example, a smiling, attentive expression, complemented by a forward lean, might portray interest and be designed to create a positive impression. That kind of behavioral pattern might appear to be indicative of an intimacy function, but it is really a managed routine designed to influence the other person. These two functions might be differentiated basically in terms of the underlying degree of spontaneity. Specifically, expressing intimacy would be relatively spontaneous and unreflective, while the social control would be more deliberate and purposeful. Furthermore, the social-control function is more likely to operate when the situation is more structured, highly evaluative, or both—for example, an employment interview or meeting with the parents of your latest romantic interest. In such situations there is a high payoff for managing one's nonverbal behavior so that a favorable impression is made.

Facilitating Service. The final category identifies bases for nonverbal involvement which are essentially impersonal. That is, the particular level of involvement does not reflect anything about a social relationship between the individuals, but only a service or task relationship. Heslin (1974) describes this type of function with respect to the use of touch. Examples of relationships in which touch is appropriate are those of physician–patient, golf professional–student, fire fighter–fire victim, and hair stylist–customer. Although high levels of nonverbal involvement are common in these and some other professional relationships, such involvement is merely the means to an end of treating, teaching, or otherwise serving the needs of an individual. Obviously, this function is not represented in everyday life as frequently as the intimacy or social-control functions, but all of us have occasion to enter such service situations.

Antecedent Factors

Although we can make some general classification of nonverbal involvement in terms of its functions, there is still a considerable variety in the initiation of different functions and in the particular forms of involvement displayed in interaction. To understand such variety we have to consider a set of antecedent factors or variables and their consequences; the first category might be described as the *personal factors*. The personal factors include those characteristics of the group or individual which contribute to nonverbal involvement.

Most important among the personal factors are *culture, sex differences, personality,* and *age.* The first three of these factors were discussed in considerable detail in chapter 6. A second general category of antecedents includes the *experiential factors.* This category identifies those past influences of special relevance for future behavior. For example, recent and similar interactions to the anticipated one will influence expectations about that interaction. An intense but negative interaction with another person (e.g., a heated argument) may lead to decreased involvement or even active avoidance of that person in the future. The third and final general category is that of *relational-situational factors.* That is, the nature of the relationship with another and the circumstances under which one interacts can considerably influence the functions represented and the level of nonverbal involvement initiated.

Mediating Mechanisms

The effects of the antecedents on the development of an interaction are assumed to be mediated by more covert processes. The first of these, *behavioral predispositions,* may be described as habitual tendencies to enact certain patterns of nonverbal involvement. That is, behavioral predispositions represent relatively stable characteristics of the individual. As such, they are more or less "automatic," requiring little cognitive input or evaluation. For example, individual differences described in the personal factors lead to some consistent tendencies for involvement. From chapter 6 we can predict that females, individuals characterized as social-approach types, and members of contact cultures generally exhibit higher levels of nonverbal involvement than persons with the opposite characteristics. *Arousal change* is a second mediating factor. The research discussed in chapter 5 indicated that more extreme changes in nonverbal behavior (e.g., close approach, touch, or sustained gaze) frequently precipitate arousal change. It appears that such arousal changes in combination with the third mediator—*cognitive assessment*—play a major role in determining the form of adjustment to another person's behavior. Arousal change and cognitive assessment mediators influence the patterns of nonverbal involvement at both the preinteraction and interaction stages of the model.

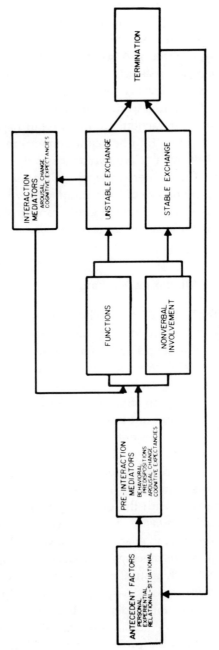

Figure 11. A diagram of the multistage functional model.

Integrating the Stages

Now that we have completed the description of the components of the model, it is time to put these pieces together in a coherent fashion. Figure 11 provides a simplified schema detailing the elements of the model and their relationships to one another.

The antecedent factors, focusing on individual differences and relational-situational constraints, provide the context for the developing interaction. As the interactants differ more on the personal and experiential factors, it can generally be assumed that those differences will be reflected in contrasting effects in the preinteraction mediators. For example, individuals from different cultures with opposing personality characteristics might be expected to have different behavioral predispositions and different cognitive expectancies about the interaction. As these contrasts in the antecedent factors and their effects on the preinteraction mediators increase, it is anticipated that the initial levels of nonverbal involvement, and perhaps even the perceived functions, will become increasingly different. This should lead to an unstable and potentially unpleasant exchange, resulting in the activation of the interaction mediators—arousal change and cognitive assessment. Then, one or both of the interactants will probably make adjustments in nonverbal involvement and possibly reevaluate the perceived function of the interaction. The adjustments likely here are those described as compensatory. For example, a too close approach by one person might result in the other person's turning away or decreasing gaze. If those adjustments are adequate, the exchange will tend to stabilize.

In contrast, as individuals are more alike or more attracted to or interested in one another, the probability increases that their expectations about one another and the interaction will be similar. This pattern of antecedent factors and preinteraction mediators increases the likelihood that similarity in perceived functions will occur and the ensuing interaction will develop in a stable fashion. In this case, adjustments are more likely to be reciprocal. For example, increased gaze and smiling by one person could be matched in kind by the other person. Regardless of the particular adjustment patterns, the termination of an interaction will produce residual effects on the antecedent factors, particularly the experiential factor.

IMPLICATIONS OF THE MULTISTAGE FUNCTIONAL MODEL

The functional model stresses that interactions, even very brief ones, can be analyzed in terms of a number of sequential stages. People bring to social situations both a variety of individual characteristics predictive of behavioral predispositions and a history of experiences relevant to the impending interaction. Furthermore, one's particular characteristics predispose a person to select specific kinds of settings and people for interaction. The combined effects of the antecedent factors are especially important in influencing arousal and cognitive mediators. As anticipated, interactions are judged to be more extreme or unusual, arousal is likely to accompany the cognitive expectancies about the interaction. Particularly important are those expectancies which might relate to one of the three molar functions described in this model: (1) expressing intimacy, (2) social control, and (3) facilitating service function.

Interactions which are guided primarily by the affective reactions (liking or disliking) toward another usually reflect the intimacy function. That is, the degree of attraction toward another is predictive of the preferred intimacy with that person, which, in turn, is manifested nonverbally. Such nonverbal involvement is relatively spontaneous and unmanaged. Of course, situational constraints represented among the antecedent factors can limit the expression of intimacy in different settings. For example, most of us are more inhibited in expressing intimacy in public than in private. Many of those circumstances affecting attraction and the way attraction is expressed were discussed in chapter 2.

In contrast, interactions which include the purpose of trying to change the reactions of the other person are more likely to involve the social-control function. If social control is primary, then nonverbal involvement tends to be less spontaneous and more managed and deliberate. Thus, if one is trying to change another person's attitude, "force" someone to comply with a request, or simply create a positive impression, nonverbal behavior can be managed to achieve such ends. A close approach, a touch, or an exaggerated facial expression might be used alone or in combination to influence another person's reaction in the desired direction. The material in chapter 3 on social influence is especially relevant for social control.

The facilitating function describes those exchanges which develop in the course of providing a service or completing a task. High levels of nonverbal involvement, as in physician–patient interactions, are not indicative of either an interpersonal affective judgment or social-influence attempts. Instead, the high involvement of a close approach, touch, and visual scrutiny are simply means to an impersonal end, in this case, completing an examination. It might be noted that in cases of such extreme but impersonal involvement, the trappings of the medical practitioner—white coat, diploma, impressive equipment, and perhaps the presence of a nurse—all signify the legitimacy of the physician's activity.

The sequential-functional perspective presented here stresses the complexity of nonverbal social behavior. Historically, discussions of nonverbal behavior have stressed the relevance of that behavior for indicating interpersonal affective judgments such as liking or love. Such an emphasis, consistent with the intimacy function, is clearly an important aspect, perhaps even the most important aspect of non-verbal behavior. Implicit in such an emphasis is the notion that non-verbal behavior spontaneously reflects those interpersonal affective judgments. However, there are other functions or purposes under-lying nonverbal behavior. Furthermore, those functions can lead to the deliberate management of nonverbal involvement with others. In formal, structured interactions and in those interactions which are highly evaluative, we are all aware that, at times, our behavior *ought* to reflect a certain attitude or reaction—and we strive to make sure that it does. Such a comment is not meant to discourage attempts at increasing sensitivity to others' behavior (and our own), but merely to sound a note of caution. With that disclaimer duly noted, let us consider some practical applications of our knowledge about non-verbal behavior.

APPLIED ISSUES

Information about nonverbal behavior and its meaning is a matter of considerable interest to most people, and for good reason. The impact of nonverbal behavior is often much greater than that of verbal behavior. We all attend to the manner in which others express ideas or feelings, and that manner may tell us more than what is actually said. In a parallel fashion, indicative of the social-control function, we often manage the way in which we converse with others. This broad interest in nonverbal behavior is certainly not lost on the authors of popular articles and books. Newspaper and magazine coverage of "nonverbal communication" is quite common. Popular books such as Fast's (1970) *Body Language* and Nierenberg and Calero's (1971) *How to Read a Person Like a Book* are avidly purchased and read in the hope of finding important applications to everyday life. The problem is that these books usually promise more than is warranted from our present knowledge of nonverbal behavior. For example, the cover of Fast's book shows a woman sitting on a plastic transparent chair dressed in a miniskirt, barefoot, legs crossed, arms crossed on her legs. Surrounding the photograph are the questions, "Does her body say that she's a loose woman?" "Does her body say that she's a manipulator?" "Does her body say that she's a phony?" "Does her body say that she's lonely?" Inside the front cover one finds: "Learn for example: How to make advances without taking chances! How to enter a room full of strangers, inventory body positions, and tell who the 'important' people are." If only it were that easy.

In spite of our skepticism about some of these how-to publications, it is clear that the relevance of our knowledge of nonverbal behavior to everyday life is considerable. We would like to concentrate our discussion of that relevance in the following areas: (1) politics, (2) intercultural relations, and (3) human-relations training.

Politics

The area of politics is one which is particularly well suited for a social-psychological analysis. Common fare in the political arena includes issues highlighting attitudes and attitude change, conformity, conflict and its occasional resolution, group structure and dynamics, and attribution processes, among others. Nonverbal behavior plays an important role in many of these processes, but it may be most important in one area—political campaigns.

Most of us like to believe that our decision making with respect to political candidates is grounded in a systematic evaluation of the candidates' relative positions on important issues. Obviously, such positions are important but—too frequently—less important than the style or manner of the candidate. An anecdotal incident reported by a fellow nonverbal researcher, Ralph Exline of the University of Delaware, is clearly illustrative of this point. He recounted his experiences during one of the televised Nixon–Kennedy debates in the 1960 presidential campaign. He happened to be driving home in the middle of one of the debates and heard it on the car radio. When he arrived home he commented to his wife that Nixon had clearly done better than Kennedy. His wife was surprised because she confidently felt just the opposite was true—from what she had *seen*. Apparently, so did millions of others.

Many political analysts believed that the televised debates provided the margin of victory for Kennedy. We saw a replay of one of those debates and the contrasts between Kennedy and Nixon were striking. Independent of one's political sympathies, Kennedy was clearly the more handsome, dynamic individual, but other differences specific to the debate setting were also evident. Kennedy looked confident and strong, and his pattern of gaze was a steady one. Nixon looked anxious and unsure of himself. He certainly appeared to need a shave. Maybe it was just a bad makeup job, but the semblance of a five-o'clock shadow did not help. In addition, beads of sweat were evident on Nixon's forehead. Last, and probably not least, was Nixon's "shifty" pattern of gaze. His eyes darted back and forth from one side to the other in rapid shifts. The contrasting images almost certainly overrode the content of their exchange.

After losing the presidential election, Nixon failed in his campaign to be governor of California in 1962. In an outburst to the news media after the election, he shouted, "Well, gentlemen, you won't have Nixon to kick around anymore." Hardly a graceful exit from politics. However, in 1968 he was back and determined not to repeat his old mistakes—and he didn't. McGinniss (1969) recounts the details of the various strategies and tactics he used to win that election. We won't go into those details, but it is clear that Nixon had a very sophisticated campaign, aimed at creating a new, positive image. This time Nixon used television to his own benefit. For example, a series of question-and-answer programs were staged with local live audiences reflecting the appropriate mixture of people from Middle America. Everything was orchestrated so that Nixon would be impressive to the television audience—even down to controlling carefully the sweat on his brow.

The 1980 presidential campaign provided a parallel to the 1960 campaign, especially in terms of the single Carter–Reagan debate. Even though Carter was behind most of the campaign, his advisers felt that a debate would certainly help the beleaguered president. The Carter camp felt that the president's intelligence, grasp of the issues, and concern for details would be too much for Reagan, who was considered to be an intellectual lightweight. This was another "sure thing" that went awry in the Carter campaign. Our own impression was that Carter probably handled the content of the questions better than Reagan. However, Reagan, the former actor, was far ahead on style points. Carter appeared to be quite tense in contrast to the smooth and relaxed appearance of Reagan. In fact, once or twice Reagan prefaced his comments with a humorous barb directed at Carter. It is difficult to tell how many people were affected by that debate, but it seems likely that Carter was not helped by it. In the visual medium of television it was naive to assume that an experienced actor would not be able to hold his own.

Whether it is these highly structured debate settings or campaigning the country in front of live crowds, much of what politicians do nonverbally can be classified as indicative of the social-control function. Managing a smiling face, showing gestures of confidence, shaking hands, patting backs, and kissing babies have as their explicit or implicit purpose the creation of a positive image. As the audience for these performances, most of us are aware of a candidate's intention to look good, but such performances still often achieve their desired ends. Obviously, this is not the case for everyone. Most affected are those who are already supportive of, or are at least neutral toward, a given candidate. Those who are strongly opposed may conveniently discount such behavior as insincere, and not representative of the "real person."

In concluding this discussion of nonverbal behavior in politics, it is important to appreciate that the management of nonverbal behavior is not limited to the campaign trail. Successful politicians usually do more than just get elected. The process of influencing their colleagues, members of business or industry, and the public between elections calls for continuous concern about managing their behavior.

Intercultural Relations

The work of E.T. Hall (1963, 1966, 1968), discussed in chapter 6, has been instrumental in sensitizing both researchers and the lay public to the importance of cultural differences in nonverbal behavior. Appreciation of these differences is especially important now that international travel has become more common and television brings distant cultures into our living rooms. In addition, diplomats, those in business, and individuals in the armed services frequently relate to people from different cultures, and the subtleties of nonverbal behavior can often determine the success of those interactions.

Most of us probably have rather biased or ethnocentric expectations about the proper way to "behave" in interactions. If those expectations have never been put to the test in interacting with people from other cultures, it is unlikely that we will be aware of them. When a person from another culture relates to us in a manner which is unusual, it is easy to label that behavior as wrong, or at least a little strange. However, if we reflect on this and try to take the other person's perspective, we realize that it is likely that he or she is making a similar judgment about our behavior. Ideally, by becoming more aware of these differences, we can avoid such evaluative judgments and adjust our behavior in a beneficial fashion.

A few examples of these cultural differences and their effects on interaction might be useful at this point. Hall's (1966, pp. 154–164) discussion of contrasts between Arabs and Westerners is particularly interesting. Arabs typically prefer close interactions, even to the point of being able to smell the breath of the other person. When a person avoids such a close interaction in the Arab culture it is a sign of being ashamed. Of course, it is not distance alone which differentiates Western and Arab behavior patterns. Related to the Arab pattern of close interactions is the preference for more directly confronting body orientations with high levels of gaze. Hall reported that an Arab friend of his was unable to walk and talk with him at the same time. Even after years in the United States, this individual could not walk along facing forward and maintain a conversation. Instead, he would cut slightly in front of Hall, turn toward him, and stop. The side-by-side position taken in walking together is considered impolite in the Arab culture. Interactions between friends require a high degree of involvement. In similar fashion, Arabs look at each other longer and more intently than do Westerners. That kind of sustained gaze in American society often has aggressive or sexual overtones and can obviously lead to some uncomfortable situations.

Another striking example is provided by Hall and Whyte. This particular incident involved American and Javanese businessmen at a cocktail party in Java. The American was seeking to develop a business relationship with a prominent Javanese and seemed to be doing very well. Yet, when the cocktail party ended, so apparently did a promising beginning. The result was that the American spent nearly six months trying to arrange a second meeting. He finally learned, through pitying intermediaries, that at the cocktail party he had momentarily placed his arm on the shoulder of the Javanese—and in the presence of other people. Humiliating! Almost unpardonable in traditional Javanese etiquette. In this particular case, the unwitting breach was mended by a graceful apology. It is worth noting, however, that a truly cordial business relationship never did develop (Hall & Whyte, 1960, p. 7).

The consequences of failing to be aware of these cultural differences can be considerable. Critical business and diplomatic exchanges may turn sour because one person has unwittingly violated a contrasting cultural norm. It might be noted that even a facile knowledge of the language of another culture cannot, in itself, prepare a person for the subtle, but critical behavioral differences.

Finally, it might be suggested that similar, though less extreme differences may be present in different ethnic or racial groups within a culture. This is especially the case in a racially and ethnically mixed society like the United States. Occasionally, conflicts arise or are exaggerated by contrasting subcultural norms for behavior. Again, it may be more important how something is said or done than what is actually said or done. The fact that differences exist at the cultural or subcultural level implies nothing about one or the other pattern of behavior necessarily being right or wrong. Appreciating that each culture's norm has both a long history and legitimacy of its own may facilitate flexibility and understanding in intercultural relations.

Human-Relations Training

Learning to recognize the importance of nonverbal behavior and its part in communication is one of the goals of human-relations training. Such training runs the gamut from rather formal courses in topics such as interpersonal communication or supervisory techniques to very unstructured groups in which learning is supposed to develop from the experience of relating honestly to other people. One critical aspect of human-relations training is that an individual needs to use immediately available information to relate effectively to others. A fair amount of that information is conveyed nonverbally. Even when people are unaware of their own reservations about some issue, that concern may still be manifested nonverbally by a lack of vocal enthusiasm, hesitation before speaking, or looking down or away while answering.

Human-relations training attempts to broaden channels of communication from a narrow verbal and intellectual range to one that encompasses the nonverbal expression of feelings. For example, at times a speaker may avert her eyes when mentioning a personal problem. In addition, her voice changes and she hesitates before finishing her comment. Although her face indicates concern, she *says* she's really not worried about it. If one attended only to what was verbalized, the meaning of that particular exchange would be lost. How does human-relations training sensitize people to be more efficient in understanding and managing such social exchanges? This general procedure focuses not only on helping participants to monitor their own nonverbal behavior (and that of others) but also on facilitating an understanding of that behavior once it is recognized.

There is no guarantee that calling people's attention to their nonverbal behavior will always be well received. Occasionally people will deny their own behavior or become upset that it is even being mentioned. However, most of the time they will welcome the fact that someone has legitimized their thoughts and provided an opportunity for discussing them. Even if the person denies a socially unacceptable feeling that leaked nonverbally, someone else present might be given the courage to discuss similar concerns. Alternatively, the invitation may be declined by everyone at that time but serve to allow people to raise the issue at some later point. Because people have difficulty getting used to an open and trusting interchange, they often need time to "take off their armor" before they can get involved in a candid discussion. If communication is to be improved, it is necessary to wed the awareness of nonverbal behavior to a willingness to address it overtly. In fact, verbalizing the nonverbal serves to facilitate the general awareness of such behavior. In this way the nonverbal behavior becomes a legitimate topic for attention.

There is another function for nonverbal behavior in human-relations workshops. Specifically, nonverbal behavior can help people experience themselves and others in new and deeper ways. We all know how we can hold others off with words, but we can often fool ourselves in a similar fashion by verbally denying what we are feeling. However, the use of nonverbal exercises can sometimes break through facades and defenses, making a person suddenly aware of his or her true feelings (Schutz, 1967, 1971). It is one thing to talk about how one feels but quite another thing to demonstrate it with another person. Nonverbal behavior can bring the experience to the person with strong intensity, capable of generating a full emotional response. That response is sometimes a surprise, even to the persons involved. For example, a man may have a very strong negative reaction to being asked to hug someone of his own sex, even as part of an exercise. The resultant anxiety, however, may help him to understand himself and his reactions to other people better.

It is clear that nonverbal behavior has a central focus in human-relations training, but what are the assumptions underlying its use? A first assumption is that facilitating a comfortable experience with nonverbal intimacy in a training group should generalize to situations outside of that group. Next, the openness and honesty stimulated by nonverbal behavior should transfer to verbal behavior. This latter assumption is grounded in the belief that one's verbal behavior, nonverbal behavior, and feelings are necessarily dependent on one another. A change in one of the components requires a related change in the others. Thus, if one expresses nonverbally some particularly strong feeling, that should facilitate *verbalizing* those same feelings.

Although, various nonverbal exercises can facilitate similar changes in feelings and their verbal expression, it is also evident that nonverbal behavior can be deliberately managed to represent reactions not genuinely felt. Positive and involved expressive reactions, such as smiling, a hearty handshake, or a hug can be managed to cover more negative feelings. Such an expressive response is characteristic of the social-control function discussed earlier in this chapter. Consequently, in concluding this section, some caution is appropriate in assuming either that nonverbal behavior always necessarily reflects internal reactions or that changes in nonverbal behavior always produce subsequent changes in feelings.

FUTURE DIRECTIONS

It seems appropriate here to speculate briefly about the direction of theoretical and applied activity regarding nonverbal behavior. First, with respect to the theoretical side, there seems to be a definite movement in theory and research toward multivariate approaches. Nonverbal expressiveness is represented in coordinated patterns involving a number of related behaviors. We can no longer afford to examine distance alone, gaze alone, or any other single behavior in isolation. A comprehensive understanding of social behavior requires attention to the gestalt provided by the integrated pattern of component behaviors. Fortunately, empirical research with a multivariate focus can be conducted relatively easily with the current availability of inexpensive videotape systems.

Obviously, the task of research is not simply to record behavior but also to try to explain and predict it. Theoretical approaches such as Cappella and Greene's (1980) discrepancy-arousal model and Patterson's multistage functional model offer more comprehensive, elaborate, and detailed explanations for nonverbal social behavior than earlier models. Of course, establishing clear support for either of these models is quite another issue. Nevertheless, a characteristic they share—which will undoubtedly be evident in future theoretical and empirical research—is an emphasis on the identification and measurement of critical mediating processes, that is, the covert events that are assumed to direct one's nonverbal reactions.

Perhaps one of the most challenging issues for future research will be pursuing the complicated relationship between verbal and nonverbal behavior. Of course, this does not reflect a simple unidimensional problem. A variety of questions must be addressed. Are the two general channels affected by the same variables in the same way? How do we weigh the relative importance of verbal and nonverbal behavior in a given situation? Do the same mediating processes (e.g., arousal change and cognitive assessment) have predictable and consistent effects on verbal and nonverbal behavior? What effect does the higher degree of awareness and control of verbal behavior have on managing nonverbal behavior? There is no dearth of important questions here.

The course for application of our knowledge about nonverbal behavior is probably more unpredictable than the course suggested for the theoretical activity. It seems likely that the general public's curiosity about nonverbal behavior will remain high. Furthermore, in almost all interpersonal endeavors, the potential is there for applying what we know about nonverbal behavior. This may extend even to important social problems. In this time of increased sensitivity to the issue of equal rights for women and minorities, there may well be attention called to the nonverbal aspects of discrimination in many institutions of society. This may be especially likely as the more overt, verbal manifestations of discrimination are reduced. Like almost any other interpersonal goal, discrimination can be facilitated by the nonverbal behavior of an individual. Because nonverbal behavior is more ambiguous and diffuse than verbal behavior, it can be denied or reinterpreted, and the offended party has no "proof" of the alleged violation. We are not in a position to offer any easy answers to this problem either, but its very existence highlights the pervasive influence of nonverbal behavior in interpersonal dynamics. Finally, in the areas of education, counseling, and therapy and in various service occupations we might expect greater attention to various experiential or training programs and activities. As in the future directions for research, the potential applications are varied and important.

References

Addington, D. W. The effect of vocal variations on ratings of source credibility. *Speech Monographs*, 1971, *38*, 242–247.

Aguilera, D. C. Relationship between physical contact and verbal interaction between nurses and patients. *Journal of Psychiatric Nursing and Mental Health Services*, 1967, *5*, 5–21.

Aiello, J. R. A further look at equilibrium theory: Visual interaction as a function of interpersonal distance. *Environmental Psychology and Nonverbal Behavior*, 1977, *1*, 122–140.

Aiello, J. R., & Aiello, T. The development of personal space: Proxemic behavior of children 6 through 16. *Human Ecology*, 1974, *2*, 117–189.

Aiello, J. R., & Jones, S. E. Field study of the proxemic behavior of young school children in three subcultural groups. *Journal of Personality and Social Psychology*, 1971, *19*, 351–356.

Alber, J. L. *Tactile communication within dyads.* Unpublished manuscript, Purdue University, 1974.

Albert, S., & Dabbs, J. M., Jr. Physical distance and persuasion. *Journal of Personality and Social Psychology*, 1970, *15*, 265–270.

Altman, I. *The environment and social behavior: Privacy, personal space, territory, and crowding.* Monterey, Calif.: Brooks/Cole, 1975.

American Psychological Association. *Ethical principles in the conduct of research with human participants.* Washington, D.C.: Author, 1973.

Apple, W., Streeter, L. A., & Krauss, R. M. Effects of pitch and speech rate on personal attributions. *Journal of Personality and Social Psychology*, 1979, *37*, 715–727.

Argyle, M. Nonverbal communication in human social interaction. In R. A. Hinde (Ed.), *Nonverbal communication.* Cambridge: Cambridge University Press, 1972.

Argyle, M. *Social interaction.* London: Methuen, 1969.

Argyle, M., & Cook, M. *Gaze and mutual gaze.* London: Cambridge University Press, 1976.

Argyle, M., & Dean, J. Eye contact, distance, and affiliation. *Sociometry*, 1965, *28*, 289–304.

Argyle, M., & Ingham, R. Gaze, mutual gaze, and proximity. *Semiotica*, 1972, *6*, 32–49.

Argyle, M., & Kendon, A. The experimental analysis of social performance. In L. Berkowitz (Ed.), *Advances in experimental social psychology.* New York: Academic Press, 1967.

Argyle, M., Lalljee, M., & Cook, M. The effects of visibility on interaction in a dyad. *Human Relations*, 1968, *21*, 3–17.

Auden, W. H. Prologue: The birth of architecture. In E. Mendelson (Ed.), *W. H. Auden: Collected poems.* New York: Random House, 1976.

Bakeman, R., & Dabbs, J. M., Jr. Social interaction observed: Some approaches to the analysis of behavior streams. *Personality and Social Psychology Bulletin*, 1976, *2*, 335–345.

Bales, R. *Interaction process analysis.* Reading, Mass.: Addison-Wesley, 1950.

Barash, D. P. Human ethology: Personal space reiterated. *Environment and Behaviour*, 1973, *5*, 67–72.

Baron, R. A., & Bell, P. A. Physical distance and helping: Some unexpected benefits of crowding in on others. *Journal of Applied Social Psychology*, 1976, *6*, 95–104.

Bass, B. M., & Klubeck, S. Effects of seating arrangements on leaderless group discussions. *Journal of Abnormal and Social Psychology*, 1952, *47*, 724–727.

Bates, J. E. Effects of children's nonverbal behavior upon adults. *Child Development*, 1976, *47*, 1079–1088.

Bauer, E. A. Personal space: A study of blacks and whites. *Sociometry*, 1973, *36*, 402–408.

Baxter, J. C. Interpersonal spacing in natural settings. *Sociometry*, 1970, *33*, 444–456.

Baxter, J. C., & Rozelle, R. M. Nonverbal expression as a function of crowding during police–citizen encounter. *Journal of Personality and Social Psychology*, 1975, *32*, 40–54.

Beebe, S. A. Eye contact: A nonverbal determinant of speaker credibility. *Speech Teacher*, 1974, *23*, 21–25.

Beekman, S. J. *Sex differences in nonverbal behavior.* Paper presented at the meeting of the American Psychological Association, Chicago, September 1975.

Berne, E. O. *Games people play: The psychology of human relationships.* New York: Grove, 1964.

Berne, E. O. *What do you say after you say hello?* New York: Grove, 1972.

Berscheid, E., & Walster, E. *Interpersonal attraction* (2nd ed.). Reading, Mass.: Addison-Wesley, 1978.

Bickman, L. The social power of a uniform. *Journal of Applied Social Psychology,* 1974, *4,* 47–61.

Bickman, L., Teger, A., Gabriele, T., McLaughlin, C., Berger, M., & Sunday, E. Dormitory density and helping behavior. *Environment and Behavior,* 1974, *5,* 465–490.

Boderman, A., Freed, D. W., & Kinnucan, M. T. Touch me, like me: Testing an encounter group assumption. *The Journal of Applied Behavioral Science,* 1972, *8,* 527–533.

Bosmajian, H. A. The persuasiveness of Nazi marching and *der Kampf um die Strasse.* In H. A. Bosmajian (Ed.), *The rhetoric of nonverbal communication.* Glenview, Ill.: Scott Foresman, 1971.

Bossard, J. H. S. Residential propinquity as a factor in marriage selection. *American Journal of Sociology,* 1932, *38,* 219–224.

Boucher, J. D., & Ekman, P. Facial areas and emotional information. *Journal of Communication,* 1975, *25,* 21–29.

Breed, G. The effect of intimacy: Reciprocity or retreat? *British Journal of Social and Clinical Psychology,* 1972, *11,* 135–142.

Breed, G., & Ricci, J. S. Touch me, like me: Artifact? *Proceedings of the 81st Annual Convention of the American Psychological Association,* 1973, *8,* 153.

Buck, R. Nonverbal communication of affect in children. *Journal of Personality and Social Psychology,* 1975, *31,* 646–653.

Buck, R. Nonverbal communication of affect in preschool children: Relationships with personality and skin conductance. *Journal of Personality and Social Psychology,* 1977, *35,* 225–236.

Buck, R. Nonverbal behavior and the theory of emotion: The facial feedback hypothesis. *Journal of Personality and Social Psychology,* 1980, *38,* 811–824.

Buck, R. W., Miller, R. E., & Caul, W. F. Sex, personality, and physiological variables in the communication of affect via facial expression. *Journal of Personality and Social Psychology,* 1974, *30,* 587–596.

Buck, R. W., Savin, V. J., Miller, R. E., & Caul, W. F. Communication of affect through facial expressions in humans. *Journal of Personality and Social Psychology,* 1972, *23,* 362–371.

Buckley, N., Linskold, S., Wayner, M., & Albert, K. *The subjective meaning of territorial invasion of human groups.* Paper presented at the meeting of the Midwestern Psychological Association, Chicago, May 1976.

Bugental, D. E., Kaswan, J. W., & Love, L. R. Perception of contradictory meanings conveyed by verbal and nonverbal channels. *Journal of Personality and Social Psychology,* 1970, *16,* 647–655.

Bugental, D. E., Love, L. R., & Gianetto, R. M. Perfidious feminine faces. *Journal of Personality and Social Psychology,* 1971, *17,* 314–318.

Burns, T. Nonverbal communication. *Discovery: The Magazine of Scientific Progress,* 1964, *25,* 30–35.

Byrne, D., Baskett, G. D., & Hodges, L. Behavioral indicators of interpersonal attraction. *Journal of Applied Social Psychology,* 1971, *1,* 137–149.

Byrne, D., & Griffitt, W. A developmental investigation of the law of attraction. *Journal of Personality and Social Psychology*, 1966, *4*, 699–702.

Campbell, D. T., & Fiske, D. W. Convergent and discriminant validation by the multitrait-multimethod matrix. *Psychological Bulletin*, 1959, *56*, 81–105.

Cannon, W. B. The James-Lange theory of emotions: A critical examination and an alternative theory. *The American Journal of Psychology*, 1927, *34*, 106–124.

Cappella, J. N., & Greene, J. V. *A discrepancy-arousal explanation of mutual influence in expressive behavior for adult and infant–adult interaction.* Unpublished manuscript, 1980.

Cary, M. S. Does civil inattention exist in pedestrian passing? *Journal of Personality and Social Psychology*, 1978, *36*, 1185–1193.

Cash, T. F., & Derlega, V. J. The matching hypothesis: Physical attractiveness among same-sexed friends. *Personality and Social Psychology Bulletin*, 1978, *4*, 240–243.

Cavior, N., & Boblett, P. J. Physical attractiveness of dating versus married couples. *Proceedings of the 80th Annual Convention of the American Psychological Association*, 1972, *7*, 175–176.

Chaiken, S. Communicator physical attractiveness and persuasion. *Journal of Personality and Social Psychology*, 1979, *37*, 1387–1397.

Chapman, A. J. Eye contact, physical proximity, and laughter: A reexamination of the equilibrium model of social intimacy. *Social Behavior and Personality*, 1975, *3*, 143–155.

Chelune, G. J. Reactions to male and female disclosures at two levels. *Journal of Personality and Social Psychology*, 1976, *34*, 1000–1003.

Clore, G. L. *Attraction and interpersonal behavior.* Paper presented at the meeting of the Southwestern Psychological Association, Austin, 1969.

Clore, G. L. *Interpersonal attraction: An overview.* Morristown, N.J.: General Learning Press, 1975.

Clore, G. L., Wiggins, N. H., & Itkin, S. Gain and loss in attraction: Attributions from nonverbal behavior. *Journal of Personality and Social Psychology*, 1975, *31*, 706–712.

Condon, W. S., & Ogston, W. D. Sound-film analysis of normal and pathological behavior patterns. *Journal of Nervous and Mental Disease*, 1966, *143*, 338–347.

Condon, W. S., & Ogston, W. D. A segmentation of behavior. *Journal of Psychiatric Research*, 1967, *5*, 221–235.

Cook, M. Anxiety, speech disturbance, and speech rate. *British Journal of Social and Clinical Psychology*, 1969, *8*, 13–21.

Cook, M. Experiments on orientation and proxemics. *Human Relations*, 1970, *23*, 61–76.

Coombs, R. H., & Kenkel, W. F. Sex differences in dating aspirations and satisfaction with computer-selected partners. *Journal of Marriage and Family*, 1966, *28*, 62–66.

Dabbs, J. M., Jr. Similarity of gestures and interpersonal influence. *Proceedings of the 77th Annual Convention of the American Psychological Association*, 1969, *4*, 337–338.

Dabbs, J. M., Jr. Physical closeness and negative feelings. *Psychonomic Science*, 1971, *23*, 141–143.

Daniell, R. J., & Lewis, P. Stability of eye contact and physical distance across a series of structured interviews. *Journal of Consulting and Clinical Psychology*, 1972, *39*, 172.

Darley, J. M., & Cooper, J. The "clean gene" phenomenon: The effect of students' appearance on political campaigning. *Journal of Applied Social Psychology*, 1972, *2*, 24–33.

Darwin, C. *The expression of the emotions in man and animals.* Chicago: University of Chicago Press, 1965. (Originally published, 1872.)

Davitz, J. R. *The communication of emotional meaning.* New York: McGraw-Hill, 1964.

Davitz, J. R., & Davitz, L. J. The communication of feelings by content-free speech. *Journal of Communication*, 1959, *9*, 6–13.

Dean, L. M., Hewitt, J., & Willis, F. N. Initial interaction distance among individuals equal and unequal in military rank. *Journal of Personality and Social Psychology*, 1975, *32*, 294–299.

Diehl, C. F., & McDonald, E. R. Effect of voice quality on communication. *Journal of Speech* and *Hearing Disorders*, 1956, *21*, 233–237.

Diehl, C. F., White, R., & Satz, P. Pitch change and comprehension. *Speech Monograph*, 1961, *28*, 65–68.

Dion, K. K., Berscheid, E., & Walster, E. What is beautiful is good. *Journal of Personality and Social Psychology*, 1972, *24*, 285–290.

Dittman, A. T., & Llewellyn, L. G. Relationship between vocalizations and head nods as listener responses. *Journal of Personality and Social Psychology*, 1968, *9*, 79–84.

Dittman, A. T., & Llewellyn, L. G. Body movement and speech rhythm in social conversation. *Journal of Personality and Social Psychology*, 1969, *11*, 98–106.

Dosey, M. A., & Meisels, M. Personal space and self-protection. *Journal of Personality and Social Psychology*, 1969, *11*, 93–97.

Duck, S. W. *Theory and practice in interpersonal attraction.* New York: Academic Press, 1977.

Duke, M. P., & Nowicki, S. A new measure and social-learning model for interpersonal distance. *Journal of Experimental Research in Personality*, 1972, *6*, 119–132.

Duncan, S., Jr. Some signals and rules for taking speaking turns in conversations. *Journal of Personality and Social Psychology*, 1972, *23*, 283–292.

Duncan, S., Jr., Brunner, L. J., & Fiske, D. W. Strategy signals in face-to-face interaction. *Journal of Personality and Social Psychology*, 1979, *37*, 301–313.

Duval, S., & Wicklund, R. A. *A theory of objective self-awareness*. New York: Academic Press, 1972.

Efran, J. S., & Broughton, A. Effect of expectancies for social approval on visual behavior. *Journal of Personality and Social Psychology*, 1966, *4*, 103–107.

Efran, M. G., & Cheyne, J. A. Affective concomitants of the invasion of shared space: Behavioral, physiological and verbal indicators. *Journal of Personality and Social Psychology*, 1974, *29*, 219–226.

Efron, D. *Gesture, race and culture*. The Hague: Mouton, 1972. (Originally published, 1941.)

Eibl-Eibesfeldt, I. Similarities and differences between cultures in expressive movements. In R. A. Hinde (Ed.), *Nonverbal communication*. Cambridge: Cambridge University Press, 1972.

Ekman, P. Differential communication of affect by head and body cues. *Journal of Personality and Social Psychology*, 1965, *2*, 726–735.

Ekman, P. Universals and cultural differences in facial expressions of emotion. In J. Cole (Ed.), *Nebraska symposium on motivation, 1971*. Lincoln: University of Nebraska Press, 1972.

Ekman, P. The universal smile, face muscles talk every language. *Psychology Today*, September 1975, pp. 35–39.

Ekman, P., & Bressler, J. In P. Ekman, Progress report to National Institute of Mental Health, Bethesda, Maryland, 1964. Cited in P. Ekman, W. V. Friesen, & P. Ellsworth. *Emotion in the human face: Guidelines for research and an integration of the findings*. New York: Pergamon Press, 1972.

Ekman, P., & Friesen, W. V. Nonverbal leakage and clues to deception. *Psychiatry*, 1969a, *32*, 88–106.

Ekman, P., & Friesen, W. V. The repertoire of nonverbal behavior: Categories, origins, usage, and codings. *Semiotica*, 1969b, *1*, 49–97.

Ekman, P., & Friesen, W. V. Constants across cultures in the face and emotion. *Journal of Personality and Social Psychology*, 1971, *17*, 124–129.

Ekman, P., & Friesen, W. V. Detecting deception from the body or face. *Journal of Personality and Social Psychology*, 1974, *29*, 288–298.

Ekman, P., Friesen, W. V., & Ellsworth, P. *Emotion in the human face*. New York: Pergamon Press, 1972.

Ekman, P., Friesen, W. V., O'Sullivan, M., & Scherer, K. Relative importance of face, body, and speech in judgments of personality and affect. *Journal of Personality and Social Psychology*, 1980, *38*, 270–277.

Ekman, R., & Rose, D. In P. Ekman, Progress report to National Institute of Mental Health, Bethesda, Maryland, 1965. Cited in P. Ekman, W. V. Friesen, & P. Ellsworth. *Emotion in the human face: Guidelines for research and an integration of the findings*. N.Y.: Pergamon Press, 1972.

Ellis, D. S. Speech and social status in America. *Social Forces*, 1967, *45*, 431–451.

Ellsworth, P. C., & Carlsmith, J. M. Effects of eye contact and verbal content on affective response to a dyadic interaction. *Journal of Personality and Social Psychology*, 1968, *10*, 15–20.

Ellsworth, P. C., Carlsmith, J. M., & Henson, A. The stare as a stimulus to flight in human subjects: A series of field experiments. *Journal of Personality and Social Psychology*, 1972, *21*, 302–311.

Ellsworth, P. C., & Langer, E. J. Staring and approach: An interpretation of the stare as a nonspecific activator. *Journal of Personality and Social Psychology*, 1976, *33*, 117–122.

Elman, D., Schulte, D., & Bukoff, A. Effects of facial expression and stare duration on walking speed: Two field experiments. *Environmental Psychology and Nonverbal Behavior*, 1977, *2*, 93–99.

Emswiller, T., Deaux, K., & Willits, J. E. Similarity, sex, and requests for small favors. *Journal of Applied Social Psychology*, 1971, *1*, 284–291.

Esser, A. H., Chamberlain, A. S., Chapple, E. D., & Kline, N. S. Territoriality of patients on a research ward. In J. Wortis (Ed.), *Recent advances in biological psychiatry* (Vol. 7). New York: Plenum Press, 1965.

Evans, G. W., & Howard, R. B. Personal space. *Psychological Bulletin*, 1973, *80*, 334–344.

Exline, R. V. Explorations in the process of person perception: Visual interaction in relation to competition, sex, and need for affiliation. *Journal of Personality*, 1963, *31*, 1–20.

Exline, R. V. Visual interaction: The glances of power and preference. In J. K. Cole (Ed.), *Nebraska symposium on motivation, 1971*. Lincoln: University of Nebraska Press, 1972, 162–205.

Exline, R., Gray, D., & Schuette, D. Visual behavior in a dyad as affected by interview content and sex of respondent. *Journal of Personality and Social Psychology*, 1965, *1*, 201–209.

Exline, R. V., Thibaut, J., Hickey, C. B., & Gumpert, P. Visual interaction in relation to Machiavellianism and an unethical act. In R. Christie & F. Geis (Eds.), *Studies in Machiavellianism*. New York: Academic Press, 1970.

Exline, R., & Winters, L. Affective relations and mutual glances in dyads. In S. Tomkins & C. Izard (Eds.), *Affect, cognition and personality*. New York: Springer-Verlag, 1965.

Fast, J. *Body language*. New York: Pocket Books, 1970.

Feldstein, S., & Jaffe, J. A note about speech disturbances and vocabulary diversity. *Journal of Communication*, 1962, *12*, 166–170.

Feldstein, S., & Welkowitz, J. A chronography of conversation: In defense of an objective approach. In A. W. Siegman & S. Feldstein (Eds.), *Nonverbal behavior and communication*. Hillsdale, N.J.: Lawrence Erlbaum, 1978.

Festinger, L. A theory of social comparison processes. *Human Relations*, 1954, *7*, 117–146.

Firestone, S. *The dialectic of sex*. Bantam Books, 1970.

Fisher, J. D., & Byrne, D. Too close for comfort: Sex differences in response to invasions of personal space. *Journal of Personality and Social Psychology*, 1975, *32*, 15–21.

Fisher, J. D., Rytting, M., & Heslin, R. Hands touching hands: Affective and evaluative effects of interpersonal touch. *Sociometry*, 1976, *39*, 416–421.

Foot, H. C., Smith, J. R., & Chapman, A. J. Individual differences in children's responsiveness in humour situations. In A. J. Chapman & H. C. Foot (Eds.), *It's a funny thing, humour.* London: Pergamon, 1977.

Forston, R. F., & Larson, C. U. The dynamics of space: An experimental study in proxemic behavior among Latin Americans and North Americans. *Journal of Communication,* 1968, *18,* 109–116.

Freedman, J. T., Levy, A., Buchanan, R., & Price, J. Crowding and human aggressiveness. *Journal of Experimental Social Psychology,* 1972, *8,* 549–557.

Freedman, N., Blass, T., Rifkin, A., & Quitkin, F. Body movements and the verbal encoding of aggressive affect. *Journal of Personality and Social Psychology,* 1973, *26,* 72–85.

Freud, S. Fragment of an analysis of a case of hysteria. *Collected papers,* Vol. 3. New York: Basic Books, 1959. (Originally published in 1905.)

Friedman, H. S., Prince, L. M., Riggio, R. E., & DiMatteo, M. R. Understanding and assessing nonverbal expressiveness: The affective communication test. *Journal of Personality and Social Psychology,* 1980, *39,* 333–351.

Fromme, D. K., & Schmidt, C. K. Affective role enactment and expressive behavior. *Journal of Personality and Social Psychology,* 1972, *24,* 413–419.

Fugita, B. N., Harper, R. G., & Wiens, A. N. Encoding-decoding of nonverbal emotional messages: Sex differences in spontaneous and enacted expressions. *Journal of Nonverbal Behavior,* 1980, *4,* 131–145.

Fugita, S. S. Effects of anxiety and approval on visual interaction. *Journal of Personality and Social Psychology,* 1974, *29,* 586–592.

Gale, A., Lucas, B., Nissim, R., & Harpham, B. Some EEG correlates of face-to-face contact. *British Journal of Social and Clinical Psychology,* 1972, *11,* 326–332.

Gale, A., Spratt, G., Chapman, A. J., & Smallbone, A. EEG correlates of eye contact and interpersonal distance. *Biological Psychology,* 1975, *3,* 237–245.

Gallup, G. G. Some chickens I have intimidated. *Psychology Today,* 1972, *6,* 62–64.

Garfinkel, H. Studies of the routine grounds of everyday activities. *Social Problems,* 1964, *11,* 225–250.

Giesen, M., & McClaren, H. A. Discussion, distance, and sex: Changes in impressions and attraction during small group interaction. *Sociometry,* 1976, *39,* 60–70.

Glasgow, G. A semantic index of vocal pitch. *Speech Monograph,* 1952, *19,* 64–68.

Goffman, E. *Behavior in public places.* New York: Free Press, 1963.

Goffman, E. *Interaction ritual.* Garden City, New York: Anchor, 1967.

Goffman, E. *Relations in public.* New York: Harper Colophon, 1972.

Gogol, N. *Dead Souls.* New York: New American Library of World Literature, 1961. (Originally published in 1842.)

Goldstein, D., Fink, D., & Mettee, D. R. Cognition of arousal and actual arousal as determinants of emotion. *Journal of Personality and Social Psychology,* 1972, *21,* 41–51.

Gottheil, E., Corey, J., & Paredes, A. Psychological and physical dimensions of personal space. *Journal of Psychology*, 1968, *69*, 7–9.

Grad, B., Cadoret, R. J., & Paul, G. J. The influence of an unorthodox method of treatment on wound healing in mice. *International Journal of Parapsychology*, 1961, *2*, 5–24.

Grantham, R. J. Effects of counselor sex, race, and language style on black students in initial interviews. *Journal of Counseling Psychology*, 1973, *20*, 553–559.

Greenbaum, P. E., & Rosenfeld, H. R. Varieties of touching in greetings: Sequential structure and sex-related differences. *Journal of Nonverbal Behavior*, 1980, *5*, 13–25.

Guardo, C. J. Personal space in children. *Child Development*, 1969, *40*, 143–151.

Guardo, C. J., & Meisels, M. Factor structure of children's personal space schemata. *Child Development*, 1971, *42*, 1307–1312.

Hall, E. T. A system for the notation of proxemic behavior. *American Anthropologist*, 1963, *65*, 1003–1026.

Hall, E. T. *The hidden dimension*. New York: Doubleday, 1966.

Hall, E. T. Proxemics. *Current Anthropology*, 1968, *9*, 83–108.

Hall, E. T., & Whyte, W. F. Intercultural communication: A guide to men of action. *Human Organization*, 1960, *19*, 5–12.

Hall, J. A. Gender effects in decoding nonverbal cues. *Psychological Bulletin*, 1978, *85*, 845–857.

Hall, J. A. Voice tone and persuasion. *Journal of Personality and Social Psychology*, 1980, *38*, 924–934.

Harms, L. S. Listener judgments of status cues in speech. *Quarterly Journal on Speech*, 1961, *47*, 164–168.

Harper, R. G., Wiens, A. N., & Matarazzo, J. D. *Nonverbal communication: The state of the art*. New York: Wiley, 1978.

Harris, V. A., & Katkin, E. S. Primary and secondary emotional behavior: An analysis of the role of autonomic feedback on affect, arousal, and attribution. *Psychological Bulletin*, 1975, *82*, 904–916.

Hartnett, J. J., Bailey, K. G., & Gibson, F. W., Jr. Personal space as influenced by sex and type of movement. *Journal of Psychology*, 1970, *76*, 139–144.

Heckel, R. V. Leadership and voluntary seating choice. *Psychological Reports*, 1973, *32*, 141–142.

Heider, F. *The psychology of interpersonal relations*. New York: Wiley, 1958.

Hendrick, C., Stikes, C. S., & Murray, D. J. Race versus belief similarity as determinants of attraction in a live interaction situation. *Journal of Experimental Research in Personality*, 1972, *6*, 162–168.

Henley, N. M. Status and sex: Some touching observations. *Bulletin of the Psychonomic Society*, 1973, *2*, 91–93.

Henley, N. M. *Body politics*. Englewood Cliffs, N.J.: 1977.

Heshka, S., & Nelson, Y. Interpersonal speaking distance as a function of age, sex, and relationship. *Sociometry*, 1972, *35*, 491–498.

Heslin, R. *Steps toward a taxonomy of touching*. Paper presented at the meeting of the Midwestern Psychological Association, Chicago, May 1974.

Heslin, R., & Boss, D. Nonverbal intimacy in airport arrival and departure. *Personality and Social Psychology Bulletin*, 1980, *6*, 248–252.

Hess, E. H. Attitude and pupil size. *Scientific American*, 1965, *212*, 46–54.

Hess, E. H. *The tell-tale eye*. New York: Van Nostrand Reinhold, 1975.

Hess, E. H., & Polt, J. M. Pupil size as related to interest value of visual stimuli. *Science*, 1960, *132*, 349–350.

Hiers, J. M., & Heckel, R. V. Seating choice, leadership, and locus of control. *Journal of Social Psychology*, 1977, *103*, 313–314.

Hinde, R. A. (Ed.). *Nonverbal communication*. Cambridge: Cambridge University Press, 1972.

Hollingshead, A. B. *Elmtown's youth*. New York: Wiley, 1949.

Homans, G. C. *The human group*. New York: Harcourt, Brace & World, 1950.

Homans, G. C. *Social behavior: Its elementary forms*. New York: Harcourt, Brace & World, 1961.

Horowitz, M. J., Duff, D. F., & Stratton, L. O. Body-buffer zone. *Archives of General Psychiatry*, 1964, *11*, 651–656.

Hull, C. L. The goal gradient hypothesis and maze learning. *Psychological Review*, 1932, *39*, 25–43.

Huston, T. L. *Foundations of Interpersonal Attraction*. New York: Academic Press, 1974.

Ickes, W., & Barnes, R. D. The role of sex and self-monitoring in unstructured dyadic settings. *Journal of Personality and Social Psychology*, 1977, *35*, 315–330.

Ishii, S. Characteristics of Japanese nonverbal communicative behavior. *Journal of Communication Association of the Pacific*, 1973, *11*, 43–60.

Izard, C. E. Personality similarity and friendship. *Journal of Abnormal and Social Psychology*, 1960, *61*, 47–51.

Izard, C. E. Personality and similarity and friendship: A follow-up study. *Journal of Abnormal and Social Psychology*, 1963, *66*, 598–600.

Izard, C. E. *The face of emotion*. New York: Appleton-Century-Crofts, 1971.

James, W. *The principles of psychology*. New York: Dover, 1950. (Originally published, 1890.)

Janisse, M. P. Pupil size and affect: A critical review of the literature since 1960. *Canadian Psychologist*, 1973, *14*, 311–329.

Jones, S. E. Homogamy in intellectual abilities. *American Journal of Sociology*, 1929, *35*, 369–382.

Jones, S. E. A comparative proxemics analysis of dyadic interaction in selected subcultures of New York City. *Journal of Social Psychology*, 1971, *84*, 35–44.

Jones, S. E., & Aiello, J. R. Proxemic behavior of black and white first-, third-, and fifth-grade children. *Journal of Personality and Social Psychology*, 1973, *25*, 21–27.

Jourard, S. M. An exploratory study of body-accessibility. *British Journal of Social and Clinical Psychology*, 1966, *5*, 221–231.

Jourard, S. M., & Freedman, R. Experimenter-subject "distance" and self-disclosure. *Journal of Personality and Social Psychology*, 1970, *15*, 278–282.

Kaplan, K. J., & Greenberg, C. I. Regulation of interaction through architecture, travel, and telecommunication: A distance-equilibrium approach to environmental planning. *Environmental Psychology and Nonverbal Behavior*, 1976, *1*, 17–29.

Kasl, S. V., & Mahl, G. F. The relationship of disturbances and hesitations in spontaneous speech to anxiety. *Journal of Personality and Social Psychology*, 1965, *1*, 425–433.

Kelly, F. D. Communicational significance of therapist proxemic cues. *Journal of Consulting and Clinical Psychology*, 1972, *39*, 345.

Kendon, A. Some functions of gaze-direction in social interaction. *Acta Psychologica*, 1967, *26*, 22–63.

Kendon, A. Review of *Kinesics and context: Essays on body motion* by R. L. Birdwhistell. *American Journal of Psychology*, 1972, *85*, 441–445.

Kendon, A., & Cook, M. The consistency of gaze patterns in social interaction. *British Journal of Psychology*, 1969, *60*, 481–494.

Kendon, A., & Ferber, A. A description of some human greetings. In R. P. Michael and J. H. Crook (Eds.), *Comparative ecology and behavior of primates*. New York: Academic Press, 1973.

Kenny, C. T., & Fletcher, D. Effects of beardedness in person perception. *Perceptual and Motor Skills*, 1973, *37*, 413–414.

Kenrick, D. T., & Gutierres, S. E. Contrast effects and judgments of physical attractiveness: When beauty becomes a social problem. *Journal of Personality and Social Psychology*, 1980, *38*, 131–140.

Kester, J. News item. *Parade*, 1972, p. 11.

King, M. G. Interpersonal relations in preschool children and average approach distance. *Journal of Genetic Psychology*, 1966, *109*, 109–116.

Kinzel, A. Body-buffer zone in violent prisoners. *American Journal of Psychiatry*, 1970, *127*, 59–64.

Kleck, R. E. Interaction distance and nonverbal agreeing responses. *British Journal of Social and Clinical Psychology*, 1970, *9*, 180–182.

Kleck, R. E., & Nuessle, W. Congruence between the indicative and communicative functions of eye contact in interpersonal relations. *British Journal of Social and Clinical Psychology*, 1968, *7*, 241–246.

Kleck, R. E., & Strenta, A. Perception of the impact of negatively valued physical characteristics on social interaction. *Journal of Personality and Social Psychology*, 1980, *39*, 861–873.

Kleck, R. E., Vaughan, R. C., Cartwright-Smith, J., Vaughan, K. B., Colby, C. Z., & Lanzetta, J. T. Effects of being observed on expressive, subjective, and physiological responses to painful stimuli. *Journal of Personality and Social Psychology*, 1976, *34*, 1211–1218.

Kleinke, C. L. Interpersonal attraction as it relates to gaze and distance between people. *Representative Research in Social Psychology*, 1972, *3*, 105–120.

Kleinke, C. L. *First impressions*. Englewood Cliffs, N.J.: Prentice-Hall, 1975.

Kleinke, C. L. Compliance to requests made by gazing and touching experimenters in field settings. *Journal of Experimental Social Psychology*, 1977, *13*, 218–223.

Kleinke, C. L. Interaction between gaze and legitimacy of request on compliance in a field setting. *Journal of Nonverbal Behavior*, 1980, *5*, 3–12.

Kleinke, C. L., Bustos, A. A., Meeker, F. B., & Staneski, R. A. Effects of self-attributed and other-attributed gaze on interpersonal evaluations between males and females. *Journal of Experimental Social Psychology*, 1973, *9*, 154–163.

Kleinke, C. L., Meeker, F. B., & Fong, C. L. Effects of gaze, touch, and use of name on evaluation of "engaged" couples. *Journal of Research in Personality*, 1974, *7*, 368–373.

Kleinke, C. L., & Pohlen, P. D. Affective and emotional responses as a function of other persons gaze and co-operativeness in a two-person game. *Journal of Personality and Social Psychology*, 1971, *17*, 303–313.

Kleinke, C. L., Staneski, R. A., & Berger, D. E. Evaluation of an interviewer as a function of interviewer gaze, reinforcement of subject gaze, and interviewer attractiveness. *Journal of Personality and Social Psychology*, 1975, *11*, 115–122.

Knapp, M. L. *Nonverbal communication in human interaction.* New York: Holt, 1972.

Knapp, M. L. *Nonverbal communication in human interaction,* (2nd. ed.) New York: Holt, 1978.

Knapp, M. L., Hart, R. P., & Dennis, H. S. An exploration of deception as a communication construct. *Human Communication Research*, 1974, *1*, 15–29.

Knapp, M. L., Hart, R. P., Friedrich, G. W., & Shulman, G. M. The rhetoric of goodbye: Verbal and nonverbal correlates of human leave-taking. *Speech Monographs*, 1973, *40*, 182–198.

Knowles, E. S. Boundaries around group interaction: The effect of group size and member status on boundary permeability. *Journal of Personality and Social Psychology*, 1973, *26*, 327–332.

Knowles, E. S. An affiliative conflict theory of personal and group spatial behavior. In P. Paulus (Ed.), *Psychology of group influence.* Hillsdale, N.J.: Lawrence Erlbaum, 1980.

Krieger, D. Therapeutic touch: The imprimatur of nursing. *American Journal of Nursing*, 1975, *75*, 784–787.

Kuethe, J. L. Social schemas. *Journal of Abnormal and Social Psychology*, 1962, *64*, 31–38.

LaFrance, M., & Broadbent, M. Group rapport: Posture sharing as a nonverbal indicator. *Group and Organization Studies*, 1976, *1*, 328–333.

LaFrance, M., & Carmen, B. The nonverbal display of psychological androgyny. *Journal of Personality and Social Psychology*, 1980, *38*, 36–44.

Lalljee, M., & Cook, M. Uncertainty in first encounters. *Journal of Personality and Social Psychology*, 1973, *26*, 137–141.

Lanzetta, J. T., Cartwright-Smith, J., & Kleck, R. E. Effects of nonverbal dissimulation on emotional experience and autonomic arousal. *Journal of Personality and Social Psychology*, 1976, *33*, 354–370.

Lazarus, R. S., & Alfert, E. Short circuiting of threat by experimentally altering cognitive appraisal. *Journal of Abnormal and Social Psychology*, 1964, *69*, 195–205.

Leibman, M. The effects of sex and race norms on personal space. *Environment and Behaviour*, 1970, *2*, 208–246.

Leventhal, H. Emotions: A basic problem for social psychology. In C. Nemeth (Ed.), *Social psychology: Classic and contemporary integrations*. Chicago: Rand McNally, 1974.

Levine, M. H., & Sutton-Smith, B. Effects of age and task on visual behaviour during dyadic interaction. *Developmental Psychology*, 1973, *9*, 400–405.

Levinger, G., & Snoek, J. D. *Attraction in relationship: A new look at interpersonal attraction*. New York: General Learning, 1972.

Libby, W. L. Eye contact and direction of looking as stable individual differences. *Journal of Experimental Research in Personality*, 1970, *4*, 303–312.

Little, K. B. Personal space. *Journal of Experimental Social Psychology*, 1965, *1*, 237–247.

Little, K. B. Cultural variations in social schemata. *Journal of Personality and Social Psychology*, 1968, *10*, 1–7.

Littlepage, G., & Pineault, T. Verbal, facial, and paralinguistic cues to the detection of truth and lying. *Personality and Social Psychology Bulletin*, 1979, *4*, 461–464.

Lott, D. F., & Sommer, R. Seating arrangements and status. *Journal of Personality and Social Psychology*, 1967, *7*, 90–95.

MacKay, D. M. Formal analysis of communicative processes. In R. A. Hinde (Ed.), *Nonverbal communication*. Cambridge: Cambridge University Press, 1972.

Maddux, J. E., & Rogers, R. W. Effects of source expertness, physical attractiveness, and supporting arguments on persuasion: A case of brains over beauty. *Journal of Personality and Social Psychology*, 1980, *39*, 235–244.

Mahl, G. F. Disturbances and silences in the patient's speech in psychotherapy. *Journal of Abnormal and Social Psychology*, 1956, *53*, 1–15.

Mandler, G. *Mind and emotion*. New York: Wiley, 1975.

Marshall, J. E., & Heslin, R. Boys and girls together: Sexual composition and the effect of density and group size on cohesiveness. *Journal of Personality and Social Psychology*, 1975, *31*, 952–961.

Matarazzo, J. D., Wiens, A. N., & Saslow, G. Studies in interview speech behavior. In L. Krasner & L. P. Ullmann (Eds.), *Research in behavior modification: New developments and implications*. New York: Holt, 1965.

McBride, G., King, M. G., & James, J. W. Social proximity effects on GSR in adult humans. *Journal of Psychology*, 1965, *61*, 153–157.

McGinniss, J. *The selling of the presidency, 1968*. New York: Simon & Schuster, 1969.

McGinley, H., LeFevre, R., & McGinley, P. The influence of a communicator's body position on opinion change in others. *Journal of Personality and Social Psychology*, 1975, *31*, 686–690.

McGinley, H., McGinley, P., & Nicholas, K. Smiling, body position, and interpersonal attraction. *Bulletin of the Psychonomic Society*, 1978, *12*, 21–24.

Mehrabian, A. Communication without words. *Psychology Today*, 1968a, *2*, 53–55.

Mehrabian, A. Inference of attitudes from the posture, orientation, and distance of a communicator. *Journal of Consulting and Clinical Psychology*, 1968b, *32*, 296–308.

Mehrabian, A. Relationship of attitude to seated posture, orientation, and distance. *Journal of Personality and Social Psychology*, 1968c, *10*, 26–30.

Mehrabian, A. Significance of posture and position in the communication of attitude and status relationships. *Psychological Bulletin*, 1969a, *71*, 359–372.

Mehrabian, A. Some referents and measures of nonverbal behavior. *Behavior Research Methods and Instrumentation*, 1969b, *1*, 203–207.

Mehrabian, A. Nonverbal betrayal of feeling. *Journal of Experimental Research in Personality*, 1971, *5*, 64–73.

Mehrabian, A. *Nonverbal communication*. Chicago: Aldine-Atherton, 1972.

Mehrabian, A., & Diamond, S. G. Seating arrangement and conversation. *Sociometry*, 1971, *34*, 281–289.

Mehrabian, A., & Ferris, S. R. Inference of attitudes from nonverbal communication in two channels. *Journal of Consulting Psychology*, 1967, *31*, 248–252.

Mehrabian, A., & Friar, J. T. Encoding of attitude by a seated communicator via posture and position cues. *Journal of Consulting and Clinical Psychology*, 1969, *33*, 330–336.

Mehrabian, A., & Wiener, M. Decoding of inconsistent communications. *Journal of Personality and Social Psychology*, 1967, *6*, 109–114.

Mehrabian, A., & Williams, M. Nonverbal concomitants of perceived and intended persuasiveness. *Journal of Personality and Social Psychology*, 1969, *13*, 37–58.

Meisels, M., & Dosey, M. A. Personal space, anger arousal, and psychological defense. *Journal of Personality*, 1971, *39*, 333–344.

Milgram, S. Some conditions of obedience and disobedience to authority. *Human Relations*, 1965, *18*, 57–76.

Miller, G. R., & Hewgill, M. A. The effect of variations in nonfluency on audience ratings of source credibility. *Quarterly Journal on Speech*, 1964, *50*, 36–44.

Miller, N. E. Experimental studies in conflict. In J. McV. Hunt (Ed.), *Personality and the behavior disorders* (Vol. 1). New York: Ronald, 1944.

Mills, J., & Aronson, E. Opinion change as a function of the communicator's attractiveness and desire to influence. *Journal of Personality and Social Psychology*, 1965, *1*, 73–77.

Mischel, W. *Personality and assessment.* New York: Wiley, 1969.

Mobbs, N. Eye contact in relation to social introversion-extraversion. *British Journal of Social and Clinical Psychology,* 1968, *7,* 305–306.

Modigliani, A. Embarrassment, facework, and eye contact: Testing a theory of embarrassment. *Journal of Personality and Social Psychology,* 1971, *17,* 15–24.

Morris, D. (Ed.). *Primate ethology.* Chicago: Aldine, 1967.

Murray, D. C. Talk, silence, and anxiety. *Psychological Bulletin,* 1971, *75,* 244–260.

Murstein, B. I. Physical attractiveness and marital choice. *Journal of Personality and Social Psychology,* 1972, *22,* 8–12.

Murstein, B. I., & Christy, P. Physical attractiveness and marriage adjustment in middle-aged couples. *Journal of Personality and Social Psychology,* 1976, *34,* 537–542.

National Commission on the Causes and Prevention of Violence, 1969.

Newman, R. C., & Pollack, D. Proxemics in deviant adolescents. *Journal of Consulting and Clinical Psychology,* 1973, *40,* 6–8.

Nguyen, M. L., Heslin, R., & Nguyen, T. The meaning of touch: Sex and marital status differences. *Representative Research in Social Psychology,* 1976, *7,* 13–18.

Nguyen, T., Heslin, R., & Nguyen, M. L. The meanings of touch: Sex differences. *Journal of Communication,* 1975, *25,* 92–103.

Nichols, K. A., & Champness, B. G. Eye gaze and the GSR. *Journal of Experimental Social Psychology,* 1971, *7,* 623–626.

Nielsen, G. *Studies in self-confrontation.* Copenhagen: Munksgaard, 1962.

Nierenberg, G., & Calero, H. *How to read a person like a book.* New York: Hawthorne, 1971.

Noller, P. Misunderstandings in marital communication: A study of couples' nonverbal communication. *Journal of Personality and Social Psychology,* 1980, *39,* 1135–1148.

Notarius, C. I., & Levenson, R. W. Expressive tendencies and physiological response to stress. *Journal of Personality and Social Psychology,* 1979, *37,* 1204–1210.

O'Neal, E. C., Brunault, M. A., Carifio, M. S., Troutwine, R., & Epstein, J. Effect of insult upon personal space preferences. *Journal of Nonverbal Behavior,* 1980, *5,* 56–62.

Patterson, M. L. Compensation in nonverbal immediacy behaviors: A review. *Sociometry,* 1973a, *36,* 237–252.

Patterson, M. L. Stability of nonverbal immediacy behaviors. *Journal of Experimental Social Psychology,* 1973b, *9,* 97–109.

Patterson, M. L. An arousal model of interpersonal intimacy. *Psychological Review,* 1976, *83,* 235–245.

Patterson, M. L. Interpersonal distance, affect, and equilibrium theory. *Journal of Social Psychology,* 1977, *101,* 205–214.

Patterson, M. L. Arousal change and cognitive labeling: Pursuing the mediators of intimacy exchange. *Environmental Psychology and Nonverbal Behavior*, 1978a, *3*, 17–42.

Patterson, M. L. The role of space in social interaction. In A. Siegman & S. Feldstein (Eds.), *Nonverbal behavior and communication*. Hillsdale, N.J.: Lawrence Erlbaum, 1978b.

Patterson, M. L. A sequential functional model of nonverbal exchange. *Psychological Review*, in press.

Patterson, M. L., & Holmes, D. S. Social interaction correlates of the MPI extraversion-introversion scale. *American Psychologist*, 1966, *21*, 724–725.

Patterson, M. L., Jordan, A., Hogan, M. B., & Frerker, D. Effects of nonverbal intimacy on arousal and behavioral adjustment. *Journal of Nonverbal Behavior*, 1981, *5*, 184–198.

Patterson, M. L., Kelly, C., & Douglas, E. A. *Walking intrusions: Proximity for a change of pace*. Presented at the annual meeting of the Rocky Mountain Psychological Association, Albuquerque, May 1977.

Patterson, M. L., Mullens, S., & Romano, J. Compensatory reactions to spatial intrusion. *Sociometry*, 1971, *34*, 114–121.

Patterson, M. L., & Schaeffer, R. E. Effects of size and sex composition on interaction distance, participation, and satisfaction in small groups. *Small Group Behavior*, 1977, *8*, 433–442.

Patterson, M. L., & Strauss, M. E. An examination of the discriminant validity of the social-avoidance and distress scale. *Journal of Consulting and Clinical Psychology*, 1972, *39*, 169.

Pattison, J. E. Effects of touch on self-exploration and the therapeutic relationship. *Journal of Consulting and Clinical Psychology*, 1973, *40*, 170–175.

Pearce, W. B., & Conklin, F. Nonverbal vocalic communication and perceptions of a speaker. *Speech Monographs*, 1971, *38*, 235–241.

Pedersen, D. J., & Shears, L. M. A review of personal space research in the framework of general system theory. *Psychological Bulletin*, 1973, *80*, 367–388.

Pellegrini, R. J. Some effects of seating position on social perception. *Psychological Reports*, 1971, *28*, 887–893.

Pellegrini, R. J., & Empey, J. Interpersonal spatial orientation in dyads. *Journal of Psychology*, 1970, *76*, 67–70.

Pellegrini, R. J., Hicks, R. A., & Gordon, L. The effect of an approval-seeking induction on eye-contact in dyads. *British Journal of Social and Clinical Psychology*, 1970, *9*, 373–374.

Porter, E., Argyle, M., & Salter, V. What is signalled by proximity? *Perceptual and Motor Skills*, 1970, *30*, 39–42.

Quick, A. D., & Crano, W. D. *Effects of sex, distance, and conversation in the invasion of personal space*. Paper presented at the meeting of the Midwestern Psychological Association, Chicago, May 1973.

Reece, M., & Whitman, R. Expressive movements, warmth and verbal reinforcement. *Journal of Abnormal Social Psychology*, 1962, *64*, 234–236.

Reed, E. W., & Reed, S. C. *Mental retardation: A family study.* Philadelphia: W. B. Saunders, 1965.

Reis, H. T., Nezlek, J., & Wheeler, L. Physical attractiveness in social interaction. *Journal of Personality and Social Psychology,* 1980, *38,* 604–617.

Reiss, I. L. Social class and campus dating. *Social Problems,* 1965, *13,* 193–205.

Rosenfeld, H. M. Effect of an approval-seeking induction in interpersonal proximity. *Psychological Reports,* 1965, *17,* 120–122.

Rosenfeld, H. M. Approval-seeking and approval-inducing functions of verbal and nonverbal responses in a dyad. *Journal of Personality and Social Psychology,* 1966, *4,* 597–605.

Rosenfeld, H. Nonverbal reciprocation of approval: An experimental analysis. *Journal of Experimental Social Psychology,* 1967, *3,* 102–111.

Rosenfeld, H. M. Conversational control functions of nonverbal behavior. In A. W. Siegman & S. Feldstein (Eds.), *Nonverbal behavior and communication.* Hillsdale, N.J.: Lawrence Erlbaum, 1978.

Ross, M., Layton, B., Erickson, B., & Schopler, J. Affect, facial regard, and reactions to crowding. *Journal of Personality and Social Psychology,* 1973, *28,* 69–76.

Rotter, J. Generalized expectancies for internal versus external control of reinforcement. *Psychological Monographs,* 1966, *80*(1, Whole No. 609).

Rozelle, R. M., & Baxter, J. C. Impression formation and danger recognition in experienced police officers. *Journal of Social Psychology,* 1975, *96,* 53–63.

Rubin, Z. Measurement of romantic love. *Journal of Personality and Social Psychology,* 1970, *16,* 265–273.

Rubin, Z. *Liking and loving.* New York: Holt, 1973.

Rutter, D. R., & Stephenson, G. M. Visual interaction in a group of schizophrenic and depressive patients. *British Journal of Social and Clinical Psychology,* 1972, *11,* 57–65.

Rutter, D. R., Morley, I. E., & Graham, J. C. Visual interaction in a group of introverts and extroverts. *European Journal of Social Psychology,* 1972, *2,* 371–384.

Ryan, E. B., & Carranza, M. A. Evaluative reactions of adolescents toward speakers of standard English and Mexican American–accented English. *Journal of Personality and Social Psychology,* 1975, *31,* 855–863.

Schachter, S. The interaction of cognitive and physiological determinants of emotional state. In L. Berkowitz (Ed.), *Advances in experimental social psychology* (Vol. 1). New York: Academic Press, 1964.

Schachter, S., & Singer, J. E. Cognitive, social, and physiological determinants of emotional state. *Psychological Review,* 1962, *69,* 379–399.

Scheflen, A. E. The significance of posture in communication systems. *Psychiatry,* 1964, *27,* 316–331.

Scheflen, A. E. Quasi-courtship behavior in psychotherapy. *Psychiatry,* 1965, *28,* 245–257.

Scheflen, A. E. *Body language and social order: Communication as behavioral control.* Englewood Cliffs, N.J.: Prentice-Hall, 1972.

Scherer, K. R., London, H., & Wolf, J. J. The voice of confidence: Paralinguistic cues and audience evaluation. *Journal of Research in Personality*, 1973, 7, 31–44.

Scherer, S. E. Proxemic behavior of primary school children as a function of their socioeconomic class and subculture. *Journal of Personality and Social Psychology*, 1974, 29, 800–805.

Schopler, J., & Walton, M. *The effects of expected structure, expected enjoyment, and participants' internality-externality upon feelings of being crowded.* Unpublished manuscript, 1975. Cited in R. G. Harper, A. N. Wiens, & J. D. Matarazzo (Eds.), *Nonverbal communication: The state of the art.* New York: Wiley, 1978.

Schulz, R., & Barefoot, J. Nonverbal responses and affiliative conflict theory. *British Journal of Social and Clinical Psychology*, 1974, 13, 237–243.

Schuman, F. L. *Hitler and the Nazi dictatorship.* London: R. Hale, 1936.

Schutz, W. *Joy.* New York: Grove, 1967.

Schutz, W. *Here comes everybody.* New York: Harper & Row, 1971.

Sereno, K. K., & Hawkins, G. J. The effects of variation in speakers' non-fluency upon audience ratings of attitudes toward the speech topic and speakers' credibility. *Speech Monographs*, 1967, 34, 58–64.

Siegman, A. W., & Feldstein, S. (Eds.). *Nonverbal behavior and communication.* New York: Halsted, 1979.

Siegman, A. W., & Pope, B. Effects of question specificity and anxiety-producing messages on verbal fluency in the initial interview. *Journal of Personality and Social Psychology*, 1965, 2, 522–530.

Sigall, H., & Aronson, E. Liking for an evaluator as a function of her physical attractiveness and nature of the evaluations. *Journal of Experimental Social Psychology*, 1969, 5, 93–100.

Sigall, H., Page, R., & Brown, A. C. The effects of physical attractiveness and evaluation on effort expenditure and work output. *Proceedings of the 77th Annual Convention of the American Psychological Association*, 1969, 4, 355–356.

Silverthorne, C., Noreen, C., Hunt, T., & Rota, L. The effects of tactile stimulation on visual experience. *Journal of Social Psychology*, 1972, 88, 153–154.

Smith, D. E., Willis, F. N., & Gier, J. A. Success and interpersonal touch in a competitive setting. *Journal of Nonverbal Behavior*, 1980, 5, 26–34.

Snyder, M. The self-monitoring of expressive behavior. *Journal of Personality and Social Psychology*, 1974, 30, 526–537.

Sommer, R. Studies in personal space. *Sociometry*, 1959, 22, 247–260.

Sommer, R. Further studies in small group ecology. *Sociometry*, 1965, 28, 337–348.

Sommer, R. The ecology of privacy. *The Library*, 1966, 36, 234–248.

Sommer, R. *Personal space: The behavioral basis of design.* Englewood Cliffs, N.J.: Prentice-Hall, 1969.

Stass, J., & Willis, F. N. Eye contact, pupil dilation, and personal preference. *Psychonomic Science*, 1967, 7, 375–376.

Stern, D. N. Mother and infant at play: The dyadic interaction involving facial, vocal, and gaze behavior. In M. Lewis & L. A. Rosenblum (Eds.), *The effect of the infant on its caregiver*. New York: Wiley, 1974.

Storms, M. D., & Thomas, G. C. Reactions to physical closeness. *Journal of Personality and Social Psychology*, 1977, 35, 412–418.

Strodtbeck, F. L., & Hook, L. H. The social dimensions of a twelve-man jury table. *Sociometry*, 1961, 24, 297–415.

Strongman, K. T., & Champness, B. G. Dominance hierarchies and conflict in eye contact. *Acta Psychologica*, 1968, 28, 376–386.

Suedfeld, P., Bochner, S., & Matas, C. Petitioner's attire and petition signing by peace demonstrators: A field experiment. *Journal of Applied Social Psychology*, 1971, 1, 278–283.

Sundstrom, E., & Altman, I. Interpersonal factors and personal space: An extension of research findings. In R. Heslin (Chair.), *Getting close: Personal space and privacy*. Symposium presented at the American Psychological Association, New Orleans, September 1974.

Sundstrom, E., & Altman, I. Interpersonal relationships and personal space: Research review and theoretical model. *Human Ecology*, 1976, 4, 47–67.

Sussman, N. M., & Rosenfeld, H. M. Touch, justification, and sex: Influences on the aversiveness of spatial violations. *Journal of Social Psychology*, 1978, 106, 215–225.

Taylor, D. A. Some aspects of the development of interpersonal relationships: Social penetration processes. *Journal of Social Psychology*, 1968, 75, 79–90.

Thibaut, J. W., & Kelley, H. H. *The social psychology of groups*. New York: Wiley, 1959.

Thompson, D. E., Aiello, J. R., & Epstein, Y. M. Interpersonal distance preferences. *Journal of Nonverbal Behavior*, 1979, 4, 113–118.

Thompson, D., & Meltzer, L. Communication of emotional intent by facial expression. *Journal of Abnormal and Social Psychology*, 1964, 68, 129–135.

Thorne, B., & Henley, N. (Eds.). *Language and sex: Difference and dominance*. Rowley, Mass.: Newbury House, 1975.

Tidd, K. L., & Lockard, J. S. Monetary significance of the affiliative smile: A case for reciprocal altruism. *Bulletin of the Psychonomic Society*, 1978, 11, 344–347.

Tomkins, S. S. *Affect, imagery, consciousness* (Vol. 1). *The positive affects*. New York: Springer, 1962.

Toomb, K., & Divers, L. T. *The relationship of somatotype to source credibility*. Paper presented at the International Communication Association Convention, Atlanta, 1972.

Trout, D. L., & Rosenfeld, H. M. The effect of postural lean and body congruence on the judgment of psychotherapeutic rapport. *Journal of Nonverbal Behavior*, 1980, 4, 176–190.

Twain, M. *The prince and the pauper.* New York: Harper, 1909. (Originally published in 1881.)

Utzinger, V. A. *An experimental study of the effects of verbal fluency upon the listener.* Doctoral dissertation, University of Southern California, 1952.

Valins, S. Cognitive effects of false heart rate feedback. *Journal of Personality and Social Psychology,* 1966, *4,* 400–408.

Valins, S. Emotionality and autonomic reactivity. *Journal of Experimental Research in Personality,* 1967a, *2,* 41–48.

Valins, S. Emotionality and information concerning internal reactions. *Journal of Personality and Social Psychology,* 1967b, *6,* 458–464.

Van Gorp, G., Stempfle, J., & Olson, D. *Dating attitudes, expectations, and physical attractiveness.* Unpublished manuscript, University of Michigan, 1969. Cited in Z. Rubin (Ed.), *Liking and loving.* New York: Holt, 1973.

Vonnegut, K., Jr. *God bless you, Mr. Rosewater.* New York: Delacorte Press, 1965.

Walker, J. W., & Borden, R. J. Sex, status, and the invasion of shared space. *Representative Research in Social Psychology,* 1976, *7,* 28–34.

Walster, E., Aronson, V., Abrahams, D., & Rottmann, L. Importance of physical attractiveness in dating behavior. *Journal of Personality and Social Psychology,* 1966, *4,* 508–516.

Walster, E., Walster, G. W., Piliavin, J., & Schmidt, L. "Playing hard to get": Understanding an elusive phenomenon. *Journal of Personality and Social Psychology,* 1973, *26,* 113–121.

Washburn, P. V., & Hakel, M. D. Visual cues and verbal content as influences on impressions formed after simulated employment interviews. *Journal of Applied Psychology,* 1973, *58*(1), 137–141.

Watson, O. M., & Graves, T. D. Quantitative research in proxemic behavior. *American Anthropologist,* 1966, *68,* 971–985.

Waxer, P. Nonverbal cues for depression. *Journal of Abnormal Psychology,* 1974, *56,* 319–322.

Webb, E. J., Campbell, D. T., Schwartz, R. D., & Sechrest, L. *Unobtrusive measures: Nonreactive research in the social sciences.* Chicago: Rand McNally, 1966.

Weisbrod, R. R. *Looking behavior in a discussion group.* Unpublished manuscript, Cornell University, 1965. In A. Kendon, Some functions of gaze-direction in social interaction. *Acta Psychologica,* 1967, *26,* 22–63.

Weitz, S. Attitude, voice, and behavior: A repressed affect model of interracial interaction. *Journal of Personality and Social Psychology,* 1972, *24,* 14–21.

Weitz, S. Sex differences in nonverbal communication. *Sex Roles,* 1976, *2,* 175–184.

Weitz, S. *Nonverbal communication.* New York: Oxford University Press, 1979.

Whitcher, S. J., & Fisher, J. D. Multidimensional reaction to therapeutic touch in a hospital setting. *Journal of Personality and Social Psychology,* 1979, *37,* 87–91.

White, G. L. Physical attractiveness and courtship progress. *Journal of Personality and Social Psychology,* 1980, *39,* 660–668.

Wicklund, R. A. Objective self-awareness. In L. Berkowitz (Ed.), *Advances in experimental social psychology* (Vol. 8). New York: Academic Press, 1975.

Widgery, R. N. Sex of receiver and physical attractiveness of source as determinants of initial credibility perception. *Western Speech*, 1974, *38*, 13–17.

Wiemann, J. M. *An experimental study of visual attention in dyads: The effects of four gaze conditions on evaluations by applicants in employment interviews.* Paper presented to the Speech Communication Association, Chicago, December 1974.

Wiener, M., & Mehrabian, A. *Language within language: Immediacy, a channel in verbal communication.* New York: Appleton-Century-Crofts, 1968.

Wiener, M., Devoe, S., Rubinow, S., & Geller, J. Nonverbal behavior and nonverbal communication. *Psychological Review*, 1972, *79*, 185–214.

Williams, E. An analysis of gaze in schizophrenics. *British Journal of Social and Clinical Psychology*, 1974, *13*, 1–8.

Willis, F. N. Initial speaking distance as a function of the speakers' relationship. *Psychonomic Science*, 1966, *5*, 221–222.

Willis, F. N., & Hamm, H. K. The use of interpersonal touch in securing compliance. *Journal of Nonverbal Behavior*, 1980, *5*, 49–55.

Woolbert, C. The effects of various modes of public speaking. *Journal of Applied Psychology*, 1920, *4*, 162–185.

Woolfolk, A. E., Abrams, L. N., Abrams, D. B., & Wilson, G. T. Effects of alcohol on the nonverbal communication of anxiety: The impact of beliefs on nonverbal behavior. *Environmental Psychology and Nonverbal Behavior*, 1979, *3*, 205–218.

Worchel, P., & McCormick, B. L. Self-concept and dissonance reduction. *Journal of Personality*, 1963, *31*, 588–599.

Worchel, S., & Teddlie, C. The experience of crowding: A two-factor theory. *Journal of Personality and Social Psychology*, 1976, *34*, 30–40.

Xenophon. *Memorabilia*. London: Heinemann, 1923.

Zimmerman, D. H., & West, C. Sex roles, interruptions and silences in conversation. In B. Thorne & N. Henley (Eds.), *Language and sex: Difference and dominance*. Rowley, Mass.: Newbury House, 1975.

Zuckerman, M., Hall, J. A., DeFrank, R. S., & Rosenthal, R. Encoding and decoding of spontaneous and posed facial expressions. *Journal of Personality and Social Psychology*, 1976, *34*, 966–977.

Zuckerman, M., Lipets, M. S., Koivumaki, J. H., & Rosenthal, R. Encoding and decoding nonverbal cues of emotion. *Journal of Personality and Social Psychology*, 1975, *32*, 1068–1076.

Index

